GOD'S INCOMPARABLE WORD

BY HAROLD LINDSELL

Published for the
**Billy Graham
Evangelistic Association**
by World Wide Publications
1303 Hennepin Avenue
Minneapolis, Minnesota 55403

Scripture quotations
in this book are taken from
The Living Bible, King James Version, and Revised Standard Version.

Cover Photo by Åke Lundberg

Library of Congress Catalog Card Number 77-92347
ISBN 0-89066-006-9, paper.
Copyright © 1977 by Harold Lindsell

MORE THAN A CARPENTER

JOSH McDOWELL

SPECIAL CRUSADE EDITION

Published for the
Billy Graham Evangelistic Association
by
World Wide Publications
1303 Hennepin Avenue
Minneapolis, Minnesota 55403

This Crusade Edition
reprinted by permission of
Tyndale House Publishers, Inc.

Library of Congress Catalog Card Number 76-58135. ISBN 0-8423-4550-7, paper.
Copyright ©1977 by Tyndale House Publishers, Inc., Wheaton, Illinois. All rights reserved. Second printing, May 1977. Printed in the United States of America.

CONTENTS

Preface

Almost 2,000 years ago, Jesus entered the human race in a small Jewish community. He was a member of a poor family, a minority group, and resided in one of the smallest countries in the world. He lived approximately thirty-three years, of which only the last three comprised his public ministry.

Yet people almost everywhere still remember him. The date of our morning newspaper or the copyright date of a university textbook bears witness to the fact that Jesus lived one of the greatest lives ever lived.

H.G. Wells, the noted historian, was asked which person had left the most permanent impression on history. He replied that if one judged a person's greatness by historical standards, "By this test Jesus stands first."

Historian Kenneth Scott Latourette said: "As the centuries pass, the evidence is accumulating that, measured by his effect on history, Jesus is the most influential life ever lived on this planet. That influence appears to be mounting."

From Ernest Renan we have the following observation: "Jesus was the greatest religious genius that ever lived. His beauty is eternal, and his reign shall never end. Jesus is in every respect unique, and nothing can be compared with him. All history is incomprehensible without Christ."

1
What Makes Jesus So Different?

Recently I was talking with a group of people in Los Angeles. I asked them, "Who, in your opinion, is Jesus Christ?" The response was that he was a great religious leader. I agree with that. Jesus Christ was a great religious leader. But I believe he was much more.

Men and women down through the ages have been divided over the question, "Who is Jesus?" Why so much conflict over one individual? Why is it that his name, more than the name of any other religious leader, causes irritation? Why is it that you can talk about God and nobody gets upset, but as soon as you mention Jesus, people so often want to stop the conversation? Or they become defensive. I mentioned something about Jesus to a taxicab driver in London, and immediately he said, "I don't like to discuss religion, especially Jesus."

How is Jesus different from other religious leaders? Why don't the names of Buddha, Mohammed, Confucius offend people? The reason is that these others didn't claim to be God, but Jesus did. That is what makes him so different from other religious leaders.

It didn't take long for the people who knew Jesus to realize that he was making astounding claims about himself. It became clear that his own claims were identifying him as more than just a prophet or teacher. He was obviously making claims to deity. He was presenting himself as the only avenue to a relationship with God, the only source of forgiveness for sins, and the only way of salvation.

For many people this is too exclusive, too narrow for them to want to believe. Yet the issue is not what do we want to think or believe, but rather, who did Jesus claim to be?

What do the New Testament documents tell us about this? We often hear the phrase, "the deity of Christ." This means that Jesus Christ is God.

A.H. Strong in his *Systematic Theology* defines God as the "infinite and perfect spirit in whom all things have their source, support, and end."[1] This definition of God is adequate for all theists, including Muslims and Jews. Theism teaches that God is personal and that the universe was planned and created by him. God sustains and rules it in the present. Christian theism adds an additional note to the above definition: "and who became incarnate as Jesus of Nazareth."

Jesus Christ is actually a name and a title. The name Jesus is derived from the Greek form of the name *Jeshua* or Joshua meaning "Jehovah-Savior" or "the Lord saves." The title Christ is derived from the Greek word for Messiah (or the Hebrew *Mashiach*—Daniel 9:26) and means "anointed one." Two offices, king and priest, are involved in the use of the title "Christ." His title affirms Jesus as the promised priest and king of Old Testament prophecies. This affirmation is one of the crucial areas for having a proper understanding about Jesus and Christianity.

The New Testament clearly presents Christ as God. The names applied to Christ in the New Testament are such that they could properly be applied only to one who was God. For example, Jesus is called God in the phrase, "Looking for the blessed hope and the appearing of the glory of our great God and Savior, Christ Jesus" (Titus 2:13; compare John 1:1; Hebrews 1:8; Romans 9:5; 1 John 5:20, 21). The Scriptures attribute characteristics to him that can be true only of God. Jesus is presented as being self-existent (John 1:4; 14:6); omnipresent (Matthew 28:20; 18:20); omniscient (John 4:16; 6:64; Matthew 17:22-27); omnipotent (Revelation 1:8; Luke 4:39-55; 7:14, 15; Matthew 8:26, 27); and possessing eternal life (1 John 5:11, 12, 20; John 1:4).

Jesus received honor and worship that only God should receive. In a confrontation with Satan, Jesus said, "It is written, 'You shall worship the Lord your God, and serve Him only' " (Matthew 4:10). Yet Jesus received worship as God (Matthew 14:33; 28:9) and sometimes even demanded to be worshiped as God (John 5:23; compare Hebrews 1:6; Revelation 5:8-14).

Most of the followers of Jesus were devout Jews who believed in one true God. They were monotheistic to the core, yet they recognized him as God incarnate.

Because of his extensive rabbinical training, Paul would be even less likely to attribute deity to Jesus, to worship a man from Nazareth and call him Lord. But this is exactly what Paul did. He acknowledged the Lamb of God (Jesus) as God when he said, "Be on guard for yourselves and for all the flock, among which the Holy Spirit has made you overseers, to shepherd the church of God which He purchased with His own blood" (Acts 20:28).

Peter confessed, after Christ asked him who he was: "Thou art the Christ, the Son of the living God" (Matthew 16:16). Jesus responded to Peter's confession not by correcting his conclusion but by acknowledging its validity and source: "Blessed are you, Simon Barjona, because flesh and blood did not reveal this to you, but My Father who is in heaven" (Matthew 16:17).

Martha, a close friend of Jesus, said to him, "I have believed that You are the Christ [Messiah], the Son of God" (John 11:27). Then there is Nathanael, who didn't think anything good could come out of Nazareth. He acknowledged that Jesus was "the Son of God; You are the King of Israel" (John 1:49).

While Stephen was being stoned, "he called upon the Lord and said, 'Lord Jesus, receive my spirit!' " (Acts 7:59). The writer of Hebrews calls Christ God when he writes, "But of the Son He says, 'Thy throne, O God, is forever and ever' " (Hebrews 1:8). John the Baptist announced the coming of Jesus by saying that "the Holy Spirit descended upon Him in bodily form like a dove, and a voice came out of heaven, Thou art My beloved Son, in Thee I am well-pleased" (Luke 3:22).

Then of course we have the confession of Thomas, better known as the "The Doubter." Perhaps he was a graduate student. He said, "I won't believe unless I can put my finger into his nail scars." I identify with Thomas. He said, "Look, not every day does someone raise himself from the dead or claim to be God incarnate. I need evidence." Eight days later, after Thomas chronicled his doubts about Jesus before the other disciples, "Jesus came, the doors having been shut, and stood in their midst, and said, 'Peace be with you.' Then He said to Thomas, 'Reach here your finger, and see My hands; and reach here your hand, and put it into My side; and be not unbelieving, but believing.' Thomas answered and said to Him, 'My Lord and my God!' Jesus said to him, 'Because you have seen Me, have you believed? Blessed are they who did not see, and yet believed' " (John 20:26-29). Jesus accepted Thomas's acknowledgment of him as God. He rebuked Thomas for his unbelief, but not for his worship.

At this point a critic may interject that all these references are from others about Christ, not from Christ about himself. The accusation in the classroom is usually that those at the time of Christ misunderstood him as we are misunderstanding him today. In other words, Jesus really didn't claim to be God.

Well, I think he did, and I believe that the deity of Christ is derived directly from the pages of the New Testament. The references are abundant and their meaning is plain. A businessman who scrutinized the Scriptures to verify whether or not Christ claimed to be God said, "For anyone to read the New Testament and not conclude that Jesus claimed to be divine, he would have to be as blind as a man standing outdoors on a clear day and saying he can't see the sun."

In the Gospel of John we have a confrontation between Jesus and some Jews. It was triggered by Jesus' curing a lame man on the Sabbath and telling him to pick up his pallet and walk. "And for this reason the Jews were persecuting Jesus, because He was doing these things on the Sabbath. But He answered them, 'My Father is working until now, and I Myself am working.' For this cause therefore the Jews were seeking all the more to kill Him, because He not only was breaking the Sabbath, but also was calling God His own Father, making Himself equal with God" (John 5:16-18).

You might say, "Look, Josh, I can say, 'My father is working until now, and I myself am working.' So what? It doesn't prove anything." Whenever we study a document, we must take into account the language, the culture, and especially the person or persons addressed. In this case, the culture is Jewish and the persons addressed are Jewish religious leaders. Let's see how the Jews understood Jesus' remarks 2,000 years ago in their own culture. "For this cause therefore the Jews were seeking all the more to kill Him, because He not only was breaking the Sabbath, but also was calling God His own Father, making Himself equal with God" (John 5:18). Why such a drastic reaction?

The reason is that Jesus said "*my* Father," not "our Father," and then added "is working until now." Jesus' use of these two phrases made himself equal with God, on a par with God's activity. The Jews did not refer to God as "my Father." Or if they did, they would qualify the statement with "in heaven." However, Jesus did not do this. He made a claim that the Jews could not misinterpret when he called God "my Father." Jesus also implied that while God was working, he, the Son, was working too. Again, the Jews understood the implication that he was God's Son. As a result of this statement, the Jews' hatred grew. Even though they were seeking, mainly, to persecute him, they then began to desire to kill him.

Not only did Jesus claim equality with God as his Father, but he also asserted that he was one with the Father. During the Feast of the Dedication in Jerusalem, Jesus was approached by some Jewish leaders who asked about his being the Christ. Jesus ended his comments to them by saying, "I and the Father are one" (John 10:30). "The Jews took up stones again to stone Him. Jesus answered them, 'I showed you many good works from the Father; for which of them are you stoning Me?' The Jews answered Him, 'For a good work we do not stone You, but for blasphemy; and because You, being a man, make Yourself out to be God' " (John 10:31-33).

One might wonder why there was such a strong reaction to what Jesus said about being one with the Father. An interesting implication of this phrase arises when the Greek is studied. Greek scholar A.T. Robertson writes that the "one" is neuter, not masculine, in the Greek, and does not indicate one in person or purpose but rather one in "essence or nature." Robertson then adds: "This crisp statement is the climax of Christ's claims about the relation between the Father and himself (the Son). They stir the Pharisees to uncontrollable anger."[2]

It is evident then that in the minds of those who heard this statement there was no doubt that Jesus claimed he was God. Thus, Leon Morris, principal of Ridley College, Melbourne, writes that "the Jews could regard Jesus' word only as blasphemy, and they proceeded to take the judgment into their own hands. It was laid down in the Law that blasphemy was to be punished by stoning (Lev. 24:16). But these men were not allowing the due processes of law to take their course. They were not preparing an indictment so that the authorities could take the requisite action. In their fury they were preparing to be judges and executioners in one."[3]

Jesus is threatened with stoning for "blasphemy." The Jews definitely understood his teaching but, we may ask, did they stop to consider whether his claims were true or not?

Jesus continuously spoke of himself as one in essence and nature with God. He boldly asserted, "If you knew Me, you would know My Father also" (John 8:19); "He who beholds me beholds the One who sent me" (John 12:45); "He who hates Me, hates My Father also" (John 15:23); "All may honor the Son, even as they honor the Father. He who does not honor the Son does not honor the Father who sent Him" (John 5:23); etc. These references certainly indicate that Jesus looked at himself as being more than just a man; rather, he was equal with God. Those who say that Jesus was just closer or more intimate with God than others need to think about his statement, "If you do not honor me as you honor the Father, you dishonor us both."

When I was lecturing in a literature class at the University of West Virginia, a professor interrupted me and said that the only Gospel in which Jesus claimed to be God was John's Gospel and it was the latest one written. He then asserted that Mark, the earliest Gospel, never once mentioned Jesus' claiming to be God. It was obvious this man hadn't read Mark—or hadn't paid much attention to what he read.

In response I turned to Mark's Gospel. There Jesus claimed to be able to forgive sins. "And Jesus seeing their faith said to the paralytic, 'My son, your sins are forgiven' " (Mark 2:5; see also Luke 7:48-50). By Jewish law this was something only God could do; Isaiah 43:25 restricts this prerogative to God alone. The scribes asked, "Why does this man speak that way? He is blaspheming; who can forgive sins but God alone?" (Mark 2:7). Jesus then asked which would be easier, to say "Your sins are forgiven"; or to say "Arise and walk"?

According to the Wycliffe Commentary, this is "an unanswerable question. The statements are equally simple to pronounce; but to say either, with accompanying performance, requires divine power. An imposter, of course, in seeking to avoid detection, would find the former easier. Jesus proceeded to heal the illness that men might know that he had authority to deal with its cause."[4] At this he was accused of blasphemy by the religious leaders. Lewis Sperry Chafer writes that "none on earth has either authority or right to forgive sin. None could forgive sin save the One against whom all have sinned. When Christ forgave sin, as He certainly did, He was not exercising a human prerogative. Since none but God can forgive sins, it is conclusively demonstrated that Christ, since He forgave sins, is God."[5]

This concept of forgiveness bothered me for quite awhile because I didn't understand it. One day in a philosophy class, answering a question about the deity of Christ, I quoted the above verses from Mark. A graduate assistant challenged my conclusion that Christ's forgiveness demonstrated his deity. He said that he could forgive someone and that wouldn't demonstrate he was claiming to be God. As I pondered what the graduate assistant was saying, it struck me why the religious leaders reacted against Christ. Yes, one can say, "I forgive you," but that can be done only by the person who was sinned against. In other words, if you sin against me, I can say, "I forgive you." But that wasn't what Christ was doing. The paralytic had sinned against God the Father and then Jesus, under his own authority, said, "Your sins are forgiven." Yes, we can forgive injuries committed against us, but in no way can anyone forgive sins committed against God except God himself. That is what Jesus did.

No wonder the Jews reacted when a carpenter from Nazareth made such a bold claim. This power of Jesus to forgive sin is a startling example of his exercising a prerogative that belongs to God alone.

Also in the Gospel of Mark we have the trial of Jesus (14:60-64). Those trial proceedings are one of the clearest references to Jesus' claims of deity. "And the high priest arose and came forward and questioned Jesus, saying, 'Do You make no answer to what these men are testifying against You?' But He kept silent, and made no answer. Again the high priest was questioning Him, and saying to Him, 'Are You the Christ, the Son of the Blessed One?' And Jesus said, 'I am; and you shall see the Son of Man sitting at the right hand of Power, and coming with the clouds of heaven.' And tearing his clothes, the high priest said, 'What further need do we have of witnesses? You have heard the blasphemy; how does it seem to you?' And they all condemned Him to be deserving of death."

At first Jesus wouldn't answer, so the high priest put him under oath. Being under oath Jesus had to answer (and I'm so glad he did). He responded to the question, "Are You the Christ, the son of the Blessed One?" by saying "I am."

An analysis of Christ's testimony shows that he claimed to be (1) the Son of the Blessed One [God]; (2) the One who would sit at the right hand of power, and (3) the Son of Man who would come on the clouds of heaven. Each of the affirmations is distinctively messianic. The cumulative effect of all three is significant. The Sanhedrin, the Jewish court, caught all three points, and the high priest responded by tearing his garments and saying, "What further need do we have of witnesses?" They had finally heard it from him themselves. He was convicted by the words of his own mouth.

Robert Anderson points out: "No confirmatory evidence is more convincing than that of hostile witnesses, and the fact that the Lord laid claim to Deity is incontestably established by the action of His enemies. We must remember that the Jews were not a tribe of ignorant savages, but a highly cultured and intensely religious people; and it was upon this very charge that, without a dissenting voice, His death was decreed by the Sanhedrin—their great national Council, composed of the most eminent of their religious leaders, including men of the type of Gamaliel and his great pupil, Saul of Tarsus.''[6]

It is clear, then, that this is the testimony Jesus wanted to bear about himself. We also see that the Jews understood his reply as a claim to his being God. There were two alternatives to be faced then; that his assertions were blasphemy, or that he was God. His judges saw the issue clearly—so clearly, in fact, that they crucified him and then taunted him because "He trusted in God...for He said, 'I am the Son of God' " (Matthew 27:43).

H.B. Swete explains the significance of the high priest tearing his garment: "The law forbade the High Priest to rend his garment in private troubles (Leviticus 10:6; 21:10), but when acting as a judge, he was required by custom to express in this way his horror of any blasphemy uttered in his presence. The relief of the embarrassed judge is manifest. If trustworthy evidence was not forthcoming, the necessity for it had now been superseded: the Prisoner had incriminated Himself.''[7]

We begin to see that this was no ordinary trial, as lawyer Irwin Linton brings out: "Unique among criminal trials is this one in which not the actions but the identity of the accused is the issue. The criminal charge laid against Christ, the confession or testimony or, rather, act in presence of the court, on which He was convicted, the interrogation by the Roman governor and the inscription and proclamation on His cross at the time of execution all are concerned with the one question of Christ's real identity and dignity. 'What think ye of Christ? Whose son is he?' ''[8]

Judge Gaynor, the accomplished jurist of the New York bench, in his address on the trial of Jesus, takes the position that blasphemy was the one charge made against him before the Sanhedrin. He says: "It is plain from each of the gospel narratives, that the alleged crime for which Jesus was tried and convicted was blasphemy:...Jesus had been claiming supernatural power, which in a human being was blasphemy''[9] (citing John 10:33). (Gaynor's reference is to Jesus' "making himself God," not to what he said about the Temple.)

In most trials, people are tried for what they have done, but this was not true of Christ's. Jesus was tried for who he was.

The trial of Jesus ought to be sufficient to demonstrate convincingly that he confessed his divinity. His judges witness to that. But also, on the day of his crucifixion, his enemies acknowledged that he claimed to be God come in the flesh. "In the same way the chief priests, along with the scribes and elders, were mocking Him, and saying, 'He saved others; He cannot save Himself. He is the King of Israel; let Him now come down from the cross, and we shall believe in Him. He trusts in God; let Him deliver Him now, if He takes pleasure in Him; for He said, "I am the son of God" ' " (Matthew 27:41-43).

NOTES ON CHAPTER 1

1. A.H. Strong, *Systematic Theology*. (Philadelphia: Judson Press, 1907), Vol. 1, p. 52.

2. Archibald Thomas Robertson, *Word Pictures in the New Testament* (Nashville: Broadman Press, 1932), Vol. 5, p. 186.

3. Leon Morris, "The Gospel According to John," *The New International Commentary on The New Testament* (Grand Rapids: William B. Eerdmans Publishing Co., 1971), p. 524.

4. Charles F. Pfeiffer, and Everett F. Harrison (Eds.), *The Wycliffe Bible Commentary* (Chicago: Moody Press, 1962), pp. 943, 944.

5. Lewis Sperry Chafer, *Systematic Theology* (Dallas Theological Seminary Press, 1947, Vol. 5), p. 21.

6. Robert Anderson, *The Lord from Heaven* (London: James Nisbet and Co., Ltd., 1910), p. 5.

7. Henry Barclay Swete, *The Gospel According to St. Mark* (London: Macmillan and Co., Ltd., 1898), p. 339.

8. Irwin H. Linton, *The Sanhedrin Verdict* (New York: Loizeaux Brothers, Bible Truth Depot, 1943), p. 7.

9. Charles Edmund Deland, *The Mis-Trials of Jesus* (Boston: Richard G. Badger, 1914), pp. 118-119.

2

Lord, Liar, or Lunatic?

The distinct claims of Jesus to be God eliminate the popular ploy of skeptics who regard Jesus as just a good moral man or a prophet who said a lot of profound things. So often that conclusion is passed off as the only one acceptable to scholars or as the obvious result of the intellectual process. The trouble is, many people nod their heads in agreement and never see the fallacy of such reasoning.

To Jesus, who men and women believed him to be was of fundamental importance. To say what Jesus said and to claim what he claimed about himself, one couldn't conclude he was just a good moral man or prophet. That alternative isn't open to an individual, and Jesus never intended it to be.

C.S. Lewis, who was a professor at Cambridge University and once an agnostic, understood this issue clearly. He writes: "I am trying here to prevent anyone saying the really foolish thing that people often say about Him: 'I'm ready to accept Jesus as a great moral teacher, but I don't accept His claim to be God.' That is the one thing we must not say. A man who was merely a man and said the sort of things Jesus said would not be a great moral teacher. He would either be a lunatic—on a level with the man who says he is a poached egg—or else he would be the Devil of Hell. You must make your choice. Either this man was, and is, the Son of God: or else a madman or something worse."

Then Lewis adds: "You can shut Him up for a fool, you can spit at Him and kill Him as a demon; or you can fall at His feet and call Him Lord and God. But let us not come up with any patronising nonsense about His being a great human teacher. He has not left that open to us. He did not intend to."[1]

F.J.A. Hort, who spent twenty-eight years in a critical study of the New Testament text, writes: "His words were so completely parts and utterances of Himself, that they had no meaning as abstract statements of truth uttered by Him as a Divine oracle or prophet. Take away Himself as the primary (though not the ultimate) subject of every statement and they all fall to pieces."[2]

In the words of Kenneth Scott Latourette, historian of Christianity at Yale University: "It is not his teachings which make Jesus so remarkable, although these would be enough to give him distinction. It is a combination of the teachings with the man himself. The two cannot be separated." "It must be obvious," Latourette concludes, "to any thoughtful reader of the Gospel records that Jesus regarded himself and his message as inseparable. He was a great teacher, but he was more. His teachings about the kingdom of God, about human conduct, and about God were important, but they could not be divorced from him without, from his standpoint, being vitiated."[3]

Jesus claimed to be God. He didn't leave any other option open. His claim must be either true or false, so it is something that should be given serious consideration. Jesus' question to his disciples, "But who do you say that I am?" (Matthew 16:15) has several alternatives.

First, consider that his claim to be God was false. If it was false, then we have two and only two alternatives. He either knew it was false or he didn't know it was false. We will consider each one separately and examine the evidence.

WAS HE A LIAR?

If, when Jesus made his claims, he knew that he was not God, then he was lying and deliberately deceiving his followers. But if he was a liar, then he was also a hypocrite because he told others to be honest, whatever the cost, while he himself taught and lived a colossal lie. More than that, he was a demon, because he told others to trust him for their eternal destiny. If he couldn't back up his claims and knew it, then he was unspeakably evil. Last, he would also be a fool because it was his claims to being God that led to his crucifixion.

Many will say that Jesus was a good moral teacher. Let's be realistic. How could he be a great moral teacher and knowingly mislead people at the most important point of his teaching—his own identity?

You would have to conclude logically that he was a deliberate liar. This view of Jesus, however, doesn't coincide with what we know either of him or the results of his life and teachings. Wherever Jesus has been proclaimed, lives have been changed for the good, nations have changed for the better, thieves are made honest, alcoholics are cured, hateful individuals become channels of love, unjust persons become just.

William Lecky, one of Great Britain's most noted historians and a dedicated opponent of organized Christianity, writes: "It was reserved for Christianity to present to the world an ideal character which through all the changes of eighteen centuries has inspired the hearts of men with an impassioned love; has shown itself capable of acting on all ages, nations, temperaments and conditions; has been not only the highest pattern of virtue, but the strongest incentive to its practice... The simple record of these three short years of active life has done more to regenerate and soften mankind than all the disquisitions of philosophers and all the exhortations of moralists."[4]

Historian Philip Schaff says: "This testimony, if not true, must be downright blasphemy or madness. The former hypothesis cannot stand a moment before the moral purity and dignity of Jesus, revealed in his every word and work, and acknowledged by universal consent. Self-deception in a matter so momentous, and with an intellect in all respects so clear and so sound, is equally out of the question. How could he be an enthusiast or a madman who never lost the even balance of his mind, who sailed serenely over all the troubles and persecutions, as the sun above the clouds, who always returned the wisest answer to tempting questions, who calmly and deliberately predicted his death on the cross, his resurrection on the third day, the outpouring of the Holy Spirit, the founding of his Church, the destruction of Jerusalem—predictions which have been literally fulfilled? A character so original, so complete, so uniformly consistent, so perfect, so human and yet so high above all human greatness, can be neither a fraud nor a fiction. The poet, as has been well said, would in this case be greater than the hero. It would take more than a Jesus to invent a Jesus."[5]

Elsewhere Schaff gives convincing argument against Christ being a liar: "How, in the name of logic, common sense, and experience, could an imposter—that is a deceitful, selfish, depraved man—have invented, and consistently maintained from the beginning to end, the purest and noblest character known in history with the most perfect air of truth and reality? How could he have conceived and successfully carried out a plan of unparalleled beneficence, moral magnitude, and sublimity, and sacrificed his own life for it, in the face of the strongest prejudices of his people and age?"[6]

If Jesus wanted to get people to follow him and believe in him as God, why did he go to the Jewish nation? Why go as a Nazarene carpenter to a country so small in size and population and so thoroughly adhering to the undivided unity of God? Why didn't he go to Egypt, or, even more, to Greece, where they believed in various gods and various manifestations of them?

Someone who lived as Jesus lived, taught as Jesus taught, and died as Jesus died could not have been a liar. What other alternatives are there?

WAS HE A LUNATIC?

If it is inconceivable for Jesus to be a liar, then couldn't he actually have thought himself to be God, but been mistaken? After all, it's possible to be both sincere and wrong. But we must remember that for someone to think himself God, especially in a fiercely monotheistic culture, and then to tell others that their eternal destiny depended on believing in him, is no slight flight of fantasy but the thoughts of a lunatic in the fullest sense. Was Jesus Christ such a person?

Someone who believes he is God sounds like someone today believing himself Napoleon. He would be deluded and self-deceived, and probably he would be locked up so he wouldn't hurt himself or anyone else. Yet in Jesus we don't observe the abnormalities and imbalance that usually go along with being deranged. His poise and composure would certainly be amazing if he were insane.

Noyes and Kolb, in a medical text,[7] describe the schizophrenic as a person who is more autistic than realistic. The schizophrenic desires to escape from the world of reality. Let's face it; claiming to be God would certainly be a retreat from reality.

In light of the other things we know about Jesus, it's hard to imagine that he was mentally disturbed. Here is a man who spoke some of the most profound sayings ever recorded. His instructions have liberated many individuals in mental bondage. Clark H. Pinnock asks: "Was he deluded about his greatness, a paranoid, an unintentional deceiver, a schizophrenic? Again, the skill and depth of his teachings support the case only for his total mental soundness. If only we were as sane as he!"[8] A student at a California university told me that his psychology professor had said in class that "all he has to do is pick up the Bible and read portions of Christ's teaching to many of his patients. That's all the counseling they need.''

Psychiatrist J.T. Fisher states: ''If you were to take the sum total of all authoritative articles ever written by the most qualified of psychologists and psychiatrists on the subject of mental hygiene—if you were to combine them and refine them and cleave out the excess verbiage—if you were to take the whole of the meat and none of the parsley, and if you were to have these unadulterated bits of pure scientific knowledge concisely expressed by the most capable of living poets, you would have an awkward and incomplete summation of the Sermon on the Mount. And it would suffer immeasurably through comparison. For nearly two thousand years the Christian world has been holding in its hands the complete answer to its restless and fruitless yearnings. Here...rests the blueprint for successful human life with optimism, mental health, and contentment.''[9]

C.S. Lewis writes: ''The historical difficulty of giving for the life, sayings and influence of Jesus any explanation that is not harder than the Christian explanation is very great. The discrepancy between the depth and sanity...of His moral teaching and the rampant megalomania which must lie behind His theological teaching unless He is indeed God has never been satisfactorily explained. Hence the non-Christian hypotheses succeed one another with the restless fertility of bewilderment.''[10]

Philip Schaff reasons: ''Is such an intellect—clear as the sky, bracing as the mountain air, sharp and penetrating as a sword, thoroughly healthy and vigorous, always ready and always self-possessed—liable to a radical and most serious delusion concerning his own character and mission? Preposterous imagination!''[6]

WAS HE LORD?

I cannot personally conclude that Jesus was a liar or a lunatic. The only other alternative is that he was the Christ, the Son of God, as he claimed.

When I discuss this with most Jewish people, it's interesting how they respond. They usually tell me that Jesus was a moral, upright, religious leader, a good man, or some kind of prophet. I then share with them the claims Jesus made about himself and then the material in this chapter on the trilemma (liar, lunatic, or Lord). When I ask if they believe Jesus was a liar, there is a sharp ''No!'' Then I ask, ''Do you believe he was a lunatic?'' The reply is ''Of course not." "Do you believe he is God?" Before I can get a breath in edgewise, there is a resounding "Absolutely not." Yet one has only so many choices.

The issue with these three alternatives is not which is possible, for it is obvious that all three are possible. But rather, the question is "Which is more probable?" Who you decide Jesus Christ is must not be an idle intellectual exercise. You cannot put him on the shelf as a great moral teacher. That is not a valid option. He is either a liar, a lunatic, or Lord and God. You must make a choice. "But," as the Apostle John wrote, "these have been written that you may believe that Jesus is the Christ, the Son of God; and"—more important—"that believing you might have life in His name" (John 20:31).

The evidence is clearly in favor of Jesus as Lord. Some people, however, reject this clear evidence because of moral implications involved. They don't want to face up to the responsibility or implications of calling him Lord.

NOTES ON CHAPTER 2

1. C.S. Lewis, *Mere Christianity* (New York: The MacMillan Company, 1960), pp. 40-41.
2. F.J.A. Hort, *Way, Truth, and the Life* (New York: MacMillan and Co., 1894), p. 207.
3. Kenneth Scott Latourette, *A History of Christianity* (New York: Harper and Row, 1953), pp. 44, 48.
4. William E. Lecky, *History of European Morals from Augustus to Charlemagne* (New York: D. Appleton and Co., 1903), Vol. 2, pp. 8, 9.
5. Philip Schaff, *History of the Christian Church* (Grand Rapids: William B. Eerdmans Publishing Co., 1962). (Reprint from original 1910), p. 109.
6. Philip Schaff, *The Person of Christ* (New York: American Tract Society, 1913), pp. 94-95; p. 97.
7. Arthur P. Noyes, and Lawrence C. Kolb, *Modern Clinical Psychiatry* (Philadelphia: Saunders, 1958). (5th ed.)
8. Clark H. Pinnock, *Set Forth Your Case* (New Jersey: The Craig Press, 1967), p. 62.
9. J.T. Fisher, and L.S. Hawley, *A Few Buttons Missing* (Philadelphia: Lippincott, 1951), p. 273.
10. C.S. Lewis. *Miracles: A Preliminary Study* (New York: The MacMillan Company, 1947), p. 113.

3
What About Science?

Many people try to put off personal commitment to Christ by voicing the assumption that if you cannot prove something scientifically, it is not true or worthy of acceptance. Since one cannot prove scientifically the deity of Jesus or the resurrection, then twentieth-century individuals should know better than to accept Christ as Savior or to believe in the resurrection.

Often in a philosophy or history class I am confronted with the challenge, "Can you prove it scientifically?" I usually say, "Well, no, I'm not a scientist." Then you can hear the class chuckle and usually several voices can be heard saying, "Don't talk to me about it," or "See, you must take it all by faith" (meaning blind faith).

Recently on a flight to Boston I was talking with the passenger next to me about why I personally believe Christ is who he claimed to be. The pilot, making his public relations rounds greeting the passengers, overheard part of our conversation. "You have a problem," he said. "What is that?" I asked. "You can't prove it scientifically," he replied.

The mentality that modern humanity has descended to is amazing. Somehow, here in the twentieth century we have so many who hold to the opinion that if you can't prove it scientifically, it's not true. Well, *that* is not true! There's a problem of proving anything about a person or event in history. We need to understand the difference between scientific proof and what I call legal-historical proof. Let me explain these two.

Scientific proof is based on showing that something is a fact by repeating the event in the presence of the person questioning the fact. There is a controlled environment where observations can be made, data drawn, and hypotheses empirically verified.

The "scientific method, however it is defined, is related to measurement of phenomena and experimentation or repeated observation."[1] Dr. James B. Conant, former president of Harvard, writes: "Science is an interconnected series of concepts and conceptual schemes that have developed as a result of experimentation and observation, and are fruitful of further experimentation and observations."[2]

Testing the truth of a hypothesis by the use of controlled experiments is one of the key techniques of the modern scientific method. For example, somebody says, "Ivory soap doesn't float." So I take the person to the kitchen, put eight inches of water in the sink at 82.7°, and drop in the soap. Plunk. Observations are made, data are drawn, and a hypothesis is empirically verified: Ivory soap floats.

Now if the scientific method was the only method of proving something, you couldn't prove that you went to your first-hour class this morning or that you had lunch today. There's no way you can repeat those events in a controlled situation.

Now here's what is called the legal-historical proof, which is based on showing that something is fact beyond a reasonable doubt. In other words, a verdict is reached on the basis of the weight of the evidence. That is, there's no reasonable basis for doubting the decision. It depends upon three types of testimony: oral testimony, written testimony, and exhibits (such as a gun, bullet, notebook). Using the legal method of determining what happened, you could pretty well prove beyond a reasonable doubt that you were in class this morning: your friends saw you, you have your notes, the professor remembers you.

The scientific method can be used only to prove repeatable things; it isn't adequate for proving or disproving many questions about a person or event in history. The scientific method isn't appropriate for answering such questions as "Did George Washington live?" "Was Martin Luther King a civil rights leader?" "Who was Jesus of Nazareth?" "Was Robert Kennedy attorney general of the U.S.A.?" "Was Jesus Christ raised from the dead?" These are out of the realm of scientific proof, and we need to put them in the realm of legal proof. In other words, the scientific method, which is based on observation, the gathering of data, hypothesizing, deduction, and experimental verification to find and explain empirical regularities in nature, doesn't have the final answers to such questions as "Can you prove the resurrection?'' or ''Can you prove that Jesus is the Son of God?'' When men and women rely upon the legal-historical method, they need to check out the reliability of the testimonies.

One thing that has especially appealed to me is that the Christian faith is not a blind, ignorant belief but rather an intelligent faith. Every time in the Bible when a person is called upon to exercise faith, it's an intelligent faith. Jesus said in John 8, ''You shall know the truth,'' not ignore it. Christ was asked, ''What is the greatest commandment of all?'' He said, ''To love the Lord your God with all your heart and all your mind.'' The problem with most people is that they seem to stop with their hearts. The facts about Christ never get to their minds. We've been given a mind innovated by the Holy Spirit to know God, as well as a heart to love him and a will to choose him. We need to function in all three areas to have a maximum relationship with God and to glorify him. I don't know about the reader, but my heart can't rejoice in what my mind has rejected. My heart and mind were created to work in harmony together. Never has an individual been called upon to commit intellectual suicide in trusting Christ as Savior and Lord.

In the next four chapters we will take a look at the evidence for the reliability of the written documents and for the credibility of the oral testimony and eyewitness accounts of Jesus.

NOTES ON CHAPTER 3

1. *The New Encylopaedia Britannica,* Micropaedia Vol. VIII, p. 985.
2. James B. Conant, *Science and Common Sense* (New Haven: Yale University Press, 1951), p. 25.

Are the Biblical Records Reliable?

The New Testament provides the primary historical source for information about Jesus. Because of this, many critics during the nineteenth and twentieth centuries have attacked the reliability of the biblical documents. There seems to be a constant barrage of accusations that have no historical foundation or that have now been outdated by archaeological discoveries and research.

While I was lecturing at Arizona State University, a professor who had brought his literature class with him approached me after a "free-speech" lecture outdoors. He said, "Mr. McDowell, you are basing all your claims about Christ on a second-century document that is obsolete. I showed in class today how the New Testament was written so long after Christ that it could not be accurate in what it recorded."

I replied, "Your opinions or conclusions about the New Testament are twenty-five years out of date."

That professor's opinions about the records concerning Jesus found their source in the conclusions of a German critic, F.C. Baur. Baur assumed that most of the New Testament Scriptures were not written until late in the second century A.D. He concluded that these writings came basically from myths or legends that had developed during the lengthy interval between the lifetime of Jesus and the time these accounts were set down in writing.

By the twentieth century, however, archaeological discoveries had confirmed the accuracy of the New Testament manuscripts. Discoveries of early papyri manuscripts (the John Ryland manuscript, A.D. 130; the Chester Beatty Papyri, A.D. 155; and the Bodmer Papyri II, A.D. 200) bridged the gap between the time of Christ and existing manuscripts from a later date.

Millar Burrows of Yale says: "Another result of comparing New Testament Greek with the language of the papyri [discoveries] is an increase of confidence in the accurate transmission of the text of the New Testament itself."[1] Such findings as these have increased scholarly confidence in the reliability of the Bible.

William Albright, who was the world's foremost biblical archaeologist, writes: "We can already say emphatically that there is no longer any solid basis for dating any book of the New Testament after about A.D. 80, two full generations before the date between 130 and 150 given by the more radical New Testament critics of today."[2] He reiterates this view in an interview for *Christianity Today:* "In my opinion, every book of the New Testament was written by a baptized Jew between the forties and the eighties of the first century A.D. (very probably sometime between about A.D. 50 and 75)."[3]

Sir William Ramsay is regarded as one of the greatest archaeologists ever to have lived. He was a student of the German historical school that taught that the Book of Acts was a product of the mid-second century A.D. and not the first century as it purports to be. After reading modern criticism about the Book of Acts, he became convinced that it was not a trustworthy account of the facts of that time (A.D. 50) and therefore was unworthy of consideration by a historian. So in his research on the history of Asia Minor, Ramsay paid little attention to the New Testament. His investigation, however, eventually compelled him to consider the writings of Luke. He observed the meticulous accuracy of the historical details, and gradually his attitude toward the Book of Acts began to change. He was forced to conclude that "Luke is a historian of the first rank...this author should be placed along with the very greatest of historians."[4] Because of the accuracy of the most minute detail, Ramsay finally conceded that Acts could not be a second-century document but was rather a mid-first-century account.

Many of the liberal scholars are being forced to consider earlier dates for the New Testament. Dr. John A.T. Robinson's conclusions in his new book *Redating the New Testament* are startlingly radical. His research led to the conviction that the whole of the New Testament was written before the Fall of Jerusalem in A.D. 70.[5]

Today the Form Critics say that the material was passed by word of mouth until it was written down in the form of the Gospels. Even though the period was much shorter than previously believed, they conclude that the Gospel accounts took on the forms of folk literature (legends, tales, myths, and parables).

One of the major criticisms against the Form Critics' idea of oral tradition development is that the period of oral tradition (as defined by the critics) is not long enough to have allowed the alterations in the tradition that these critics have alleged. Speaking of the brevity of the time element involved in the writing of the New Testament, Simon Kistemaker, professor of Bible at Dordt College, writes: "Normally, the accumulation of folklore among people of primitive culture takes many generations; it is a gradual process spread over centuries of time. But in conformity with the thinking of the form critic, we must conclude that the Gospel stories were produced and collected within little more than one generation. In terms of the form-critical approach, the formation of the individual Gospel units must be understood as a telescoped project with accelerated course of action."[6]

A.H. McNeile, former Regius Professor of Divinity at the University of Dublin, challenges Form Criticism's concept of oral tradition. He points out that Form Critics do not deal with the tradition of Jesus' words as closely as they should. A careful look at 1 Corinthians 7:10,12,25 shows the careful preservation and the existence of a genuine tradition of recording these words. In the Jewish religion it was customary for a student to memorize a rabbi's teaching. A good pupil was like "a plastered cistern that loses not a drop" (Mishna, Aboth, ii, 8). If we rely on C.F. Burney's theory (in *The Poetry of Our Lord*, 1925), we can assume that much of the Lord's teaching is in Aramaic poetical form, making it easy to be memorized.[7]

Paul L. Maier, professor of ancient history at Western Michigan University, writes: "Arguments that Christianity hatched its Easter myth over a lengthy period of time or that the sources were written many years after the event are simply not factual."[8] Analyzing Form Criticism, Albright wrote: "Only modern scholars who lack both historical method and perspective can spin such a web of speculation as that with which form critics have surrounded the Gospel tradition." Albright's own conclusion was that "a period of twenty to fifty years is too slight to permit of any appreciable corruption of the essential content and even of the specific wording of the sayings of Jesus."[9]

Often when I am talking with someone about the Bible they sarcastically reply that you can't trust what the Bible says. Why, it was written almost 2,000 years ago. It's full of errors and discrepancies. I reply that I believe I *can* trust the Scriptures. Then I describe an incident that took place during a lecture in a history class. I made the statement that I believed there was more evidence for the reliability of the New Testament than for almost any ten pieces of classical literature put together. The professor sat over in the corner snickering, as if to say, "Oh, gee—come on." I said, "What are you snickering about?" He said, "The audacity to make the statement in a history class that the New Testament is reliable. That's ridiculous." Well, I appreciate it when somebody makes a statement like that because I always like to ask this one question. (I've never had a positive response.) I said, "Tell me, sir, as a historian, what are the tests that you apply to any piece of literature of history to determine if it's accurate or reliable?" The amazing thing was he didn't have any tests. I answered, "I have some tests." I believe that the historical reliability of the Scripture should be tested by the same criteria that all historical documents are tested by. Military historian C. Sanders lists and explains the three basic principles of historiography. They are the bibliographical test, the internal evidence test, and the external evidence test.[10]

BIBLIOGRAPHICAL TEST

The bibliographical test is an examination of the textual transmission by which documents reach us. In other words, not having the original documents, how reliable are the copies we have in regard to the number of manuscripts (MSS) and the time interval between the original and extant copy?

We can appreciate the tremendous wealth of manuscript authority of the New Testament by comparing it with textual material from other notable ancient sources.

The history of Thucydides (460-400 B.C.) is available to us from just eight MSS dated about A.D. 900, almost 1,300 years after he wrote. The MSS of the history of Herodotus are likewise late and scarce, and yet, as F.F. Bruce concludes, "No classical scholar would listen to an argument that the authenticity of Herodotus or Thucydides is in doubt because the earliest manuscripts of their works which are of use to us are over 1,300 years later than the originals."[11]

Aristotle wrote his poetics around 343 B.C. and yet the earliest copy we have is dated A.D. 1100, nearly a 1,400-year gap, and only five MSS are in existence.

Caesar composed his history of the Gallic Wars between 58 and 50 B.C. and its manuscript authority rests on nine or ten copies dating 1,000 years after his death.

When it comes to the manuscript authority of the New Testament, the abundance of material is almost embarrassing in contrast. After the early papyri manuscript discoveries that bridged the gap between the times of Christ and the second century, an abundance of other MSS came to light. Over 20,000 copies of New Testament manuscripts are in existence today. The *Iliad* has 643 MSS and is second in manuscript authority after the New Testament.

Sir Frederic Kenyon, who was the director and principal librarian at the British Museum and second to none in authority in issuing statements about manuscripts, concludes: "The interval then between the dates of original composition and the earliest extant evidence becomes so small as to be in fact negligible, and the last foundation for any doubt that the Scriptures have come down to us substancially as they were written has now been removed. Both the authenticity and the general integrity of the books of the New Testament may be regarded as finally established."[12]

The New Testament Greek scholar J. Harold Greenlee adds: "Since scholars accept as generally trustworthy the writings of the ancient classics even though the earliest MSS were written so long after the original writings and the number of extant MSS is in many instances so small, it is clear that the reliability of the text of the New Testament is likewise assured."[13]

The application of the bibliographical test to the New Testament assures us that it has more manuscript authority than any piece of literature from antiquity. Adding to that authority the more than 100 years of intensive New Testament textual criticism, one can conclude that an authentic New Testament text has been established.

INTERNAL EVIDENCE TEST

The bibliographical test has determined only that the text we have now is what was originally recorded. One has still to determine whether that written record is credible and to what extent. That is the problem of internal criticism, which is the second test of historicity listed by C. Sanders.

At this point the literary critic still follows Aristotle's dictum: "The benefit of the doubt is to be given to the document itself, and not arrogated by the critic to himself." In other words, as John W. Montgomery summarizes: "One must listen to the claims of the document under analysis, and not assume fraud or error unless the author disqualified himself by contradictions or known factual inaccuracies."[14]

Dr. Louis Gottschalk, former professor of history at the University of Chicago, outlines his historical method in a guide used by many for historical investigation. Gottschalk points out that the ability of the writer or the witness to tell the truth is helpful to the historian to determine credibility, "even if it is contained in a document obtained by force or fraud, or is otherwise impeachable, or is based on hearsay evidence, or is from an interested witness."[15]

This "ability to tell the truth" is closely related to the witness's nearness both geographically and chronologically to the events recorded. The New Testament accounts of the life and teaching of Jesus were recorded by men who had been either eyewitnesses themselves or who related the accounts of eyewitnesses of the actual events or teachings of Christ.

Luke 1:1-3—"Inasmuch as many have undertaken to compile an account of the things accomplished among us, just as those who from the beginning were eyewitnesses and servants of the Word have handed them down to us, it seemed fitting for me as well, having investigated everything carefully from the beginning, to write it out for you in consecutive order, most excellent Theophilus."

2 Peter 1:16—"For we did not follow cleverly devised tales when we made known to you the power and coming of our Lord Jesus Christ, but we were eyewitnesses of His majesty."

1 John 1:3—"...what we have seen and heard we proclaim to you also, that you also may have fellowship with us; and indeed our fellowship is with the Father, and with His Son Jesus Christ."

John 19:35—"And he who has seen has borne witness, and his witness is true; and he knows that he is telling the truth, so that you also may believe."

Luke 3:1—"Now in the fifteenth year of the reign of Tiberius Caesar, when Pontius Pilate was governor of Judea, and Herod was tetrarch of Galilee, and his brother Phillip was tetrarch of the region of Ituraea and Trachonitis, and Lysanias was tetrarch of Abilene..."

This closeness to the recorded accounts is an extremely effective means of certifying the accuracy of what is retained by a witness. The historian, however, also has to deal with the eyewitness who consciously or unconsciously tells falsehoods even though he is near to the event and is competent to tell the truth.

The New Testament accounts of Christ were being circulated within the lifetimes of those alive at the time of his life. These people could certainly confirm or deny the accuracy of the accounts. In advocating their case for the gospel, the apostles had appealed (even when confronting their most severe opponents) to common knowledge concerning Jesus. They not only said, "Look, we saw this" or

"We heard that..." but they turned the tables around and right in front of adverse critics said, "You also know about these things... You saw them; you yourselves know about it." One had better be careful when he says to his opposition, "You know this also, " because if he isn't right in the details, it will be shoved right back down his throat.

Acts 2:22—"Men of Israel, listen to these words: Jesus the Nazarene, a man attested to you by God with miracles and wonders and signs which God performed through Him in your midst, just as you yourselves know..."

Acts 26:24-28—"And while Paul was saying this in his defense, Festus said in a loud voice, 'Paul, you are out of your mind! Your great learning is driving you mad.' But Paul said, 'I am not out of my mind, most excellent Festus, but I utter words of sober truth. For the king knows about these matters, and I speak to him also with confidence, since I am persuaded that none of these things escape his notice; for this has not been done in a corner.' "

Concerning the primary-source value of the New Testament records, F.F. Bruce, Rylands Professor of Biblical Criticism and Exegesis at the University of Manchester, says: "And it was not only friendly eyewitnesses that the early preachers had to reckon with; there were others less well disposed who were also conversant with the main facts of the ministry and death of Jesus. The disciples could not afford to risk inaccuracies (not to speak of willful manipulation of the facts), which would at once be exposed by those who would be only too glad to do so. On the contrary, one of the strong points in the original apostolic preaching is the confident appeal to the knowledge of the hearers; they not only said, 'We are witnesses of these things,' but also, 'As you yourselves also know' (Acts 2:22). Had there been any tendency to depart from the facts in any material respect, the possible presence of hostile witnesses in the audience would have served as a further corrective."[11]

Lawrence J. McGinley of Saint Peter's College comments on the value of hostile witnesses in relationship to recorded events: "First of all, eyewitnesses of the events in question were still alive when the tradition had been completely formed; and among those eyewitnesses were bitter enemies of the new religious movement. Yet the tradition claimed to narrate a series of well-known deeds and publicly taught doctrines at a time when false statements could, and would, be challenged."[16]

New Testament scholar Robert Grant of the University of Chicago concludes: "At the time they [the synoptic gospels] were written or may be supposed to have been written, there were eyewitnesses and their testimony was not completely disregarded...This means that the gospels must be regarded as largely reliable witnesses to the life, death, and resurrection of Jesus."[17]

Will Durant, who was trained in the discipline of historical investigation and spent his life analyzing records of antiquity, writes: "Despite the prejudices and theological preconceptions of the evangelists, they record many incidents that mere inventors would have concealed—the competition of the apostles for high places in the Kingdom, their flight after Jesus' arrest, Peter's denial, the failure of Christ to work miracles in Galilee, the references of some auditors to his possible insanity, his early uncertainty as to his mission, his confessions of ignorance as to the future, his moments of bitterness, his despairing cry on the cross; no one reading these scenes can doubt the reality of the figure behind them. That a few simple men should in one generation have invented so powerful and appealing a personality, so lofty an ethic, and so inspiring a vision of human brotherhood, would be a miracle far more incredible than any recorded in the Gospels. After two centuries of Higher Criticism the outlines of the life, character, and teaching of Christ remain reasonably clear, and constitute the most fascinating feature in the history of Western man."[18]

EXTERNAL EVIDENCE TEST

The third test of historicity is that of external evidence. The issue here is whether other historical material confirms or denies the internal testimony of the documents themselves. In other words, what sources are there, apart from the literature under analysis that substantiate its accuracy, reliability, and authenticity?

Gottschalk argues that "*conformity* or *agreement* with other known historical or scientific facts is often the decisive test of evidence, whether of one or of more witnesses."[15]

Two friends of the Apostle John confirm the internal evidence from John's accounts. The historian Eusebius preserves writings of Papias, bishop of Hierapolis (A.D. 130): "The Elder [Apostle John] used to say this also: 'Mark, having been the interpreter of Peter, wrote down accurately all that he [Peter] mentioned, whether sayings or doings of Christ, not, however, in order. For he was neither a hearer nor a companion of the Lord; but afterwards, as I said, he accompanied Peter, who adapted his teachings as necessity required, not as though he were making a compilation of the sayings of the Lord. So then Mark made no mistake, writing down in this way some things as he mentioned them; for he paid attention to this one thing, not to omit anything that he had heard, not to include any false statement among them.' "[19]

Irenaeus, Bishop of Lyons (A.D. 180. Irenaeus was a student of Polycarp, Bishop of Smyrna, who had been a Christian for eighty-six years, and was a disciple of John the Apostle) wrote: "Matthew published his Gospel among the Hebrews [i.e., Jews] in their own tongue, when Peter and Paul were preaching the gospel in Rome and founding the church there. After their departure [i.e., death, which strong tradition places at the time of the Neronian persecution in 64], Mark, the disciple and interpreter of Peter, himself handed down to us in writing the substance of Peter's preaching. Luke the follower of Paul, set down in a book the gospel preached by his teacher. Then John, the disciple of the Lord, who also leaned on his breast [this is a reference to John 13:25 and 21:20], himself produced his Gospel, while he was living at Ephesus in Asia."[20]

Archaeology often provides powerful external evidence. It contributes to biblical criticism, not in the area of inspiration and revelation, but by providing evidence of accuracy about events that are recorded. Archaeologist Joseph Free writes: "Archaeology has confirmed countless passages which have been rejected by critics as unhistorical or contradictory to known facts."[21]

We have already seen how archaeology caused Sir William Ramsay to change his initial negative convictions about the historicity of Luke and come to the conclusion that the Book of Acts was accurate in its description of the geography, antiquities, and society of Asia Minor.

F.F. Bruce notes that "where Luke has been suspected of inaccuracy, and accuracy has been vindicated by some inscriptional [external] evidence, it may be legitimate to say that archaeology has confirmed the New Testament record."[22]

A.N. Sherwin-White, a classical historian, writes that "for Acts the confirmation of historicity is overwhelming." He continues by saying that "any attempt to reject its basic historicity even in matters of detail must now appear absurd. Roman historians have long taken it for granted."[23]

After personally trying to shatter the historicity and validity of the Scriptures, I have come to the conclusion that they are historically trustworthy. If a person discards the Bible as unreliable in this sense, then he or she must discard almost all the literature of antiquity. One problem I constantly face is the desire on the part of many to apply one standard or test to secular literature and another to the Bible. We need to apply the same test, whether the literature under investigation is secular or religious. Having done this, I believe we can say, "The Bible is trustworthy and historically reliable in its witness about Jesus."

Dr. Clark H. Pinnock, professor of systematic theology at Regent College, states: "There exists no document from the ancient world witnessed by so excellent a set of textual and historical testimonies, and offering so superb an array of historical data on which an intelligent decision may be made. An honest [person] cannot dismiss a source of this kind. Skepticism regarding the historical credentials of Christianity is based upon an irrational [i.e., antisupernatural] bias."[24]

NOTES ON CHAPTER 4

1. Millar Burrows, *What Mean These Stones*. (New York: Meridian Books, 1956), p. 52.
2. William F. Albright, *Recent Discoveries in Bible Lands*. (New York: Funk and Wagnalls, 1955), p. 136.
3. William F. Albright, *Christianity Today*, Vol. 7, Jan. 18, 1963, p. 3.
4. Sir William Ramsay, *The Bearing of Recent Discovery on the Trustworthiness of the New Testament*. (London: Hodder and Stoughton, 1915;, p. 222.
5. John A.T. Robinson, *Redating the New Testament* (London: SCM Press, 1976).
6. Simon Kistemaker, *The Gospels in Current Study*. (Grand Rapids: Baker Book House, 1972), pp. 48-49.
7. A.H. McNeile, *An Introduction to the Study of the New Testament*. (London: Oxford University Press, 1953), p. 54.
8. Paul L. Maier, *First Easter: The True and Unfamiliar Story*. (New York: Harper and Row, 1973), p. 122.
9. William F. Albright, *From the Stone Age to Christianity* (second edition). (Baltimore: Johns Hopkins Press, 1946), pp. 297, 298.
10. C. Sanders, *Introduction to Research in English Literary History*. (New York: MacMillan Company, 1952), pp. 143 ff.
11. F.F. Bruce, *The New Testament Documents: Are They Reliable?* (Downers Grove, Ill. 60515: Inter Varsity Press, 1964), pp. 16 f.; p. 33.
12. Sir Frederic Kenyon, *The Bible and Archaeology*. (New York: Harper and Row, 1940), pp. 288, 289.
13. J. Harold Greenlee, *Introduction to New Testament Textual Criticism* (Grand Rapids: William B. Eerdmans Publishing Company, 1964), p. 16.
14. John Warwick Montgomery, *History and Christianity* (Downers Grove, Ill.: InterVarsity Press, 1971), p. 29.
15. Louis R. Gottschalk, *Understanding History* (New York: Knopf, 1969, 2nd ed), p. 150; p. 161; p. 168.
16. Lawrence J. McGinley, *Form Criticism of the Synoptic Healing Narratives* Woodstock, Maryland: Woodstock College Press, 1944), p. 25.
17. Robert Grant, *Historical Introduction to the New Testament* (New York: Harper and Row, 1963), p. 302.

18. Will Durant, *Caesar and Christ,* in *The Story of Civilization,* Vol. 3. (New York: Simon & Schuster, 1944), p. 557.

19. Eusebius. *Ecclesiastical History,* Book 3, Chapter 39.

20. Irenaeus. *Against Heresies.* 3.1.1.

21. Joseph Free, *Archaeology and Bible History* (Wheaton, Ill: Scripture Press, 1969), p. 1.

22. F.F. Bruce, "Archaeological Confirmation of the New Testament," in *Revelation and the Bible.* Edited by Carl Henry. (Grand Rapids: Baker Book House, 1969), p. 331.

23. A.N. Sherwin-White, *Roman Society and Roman Law in the New Testament* (Oxford: Clarendon Press, 1963), p. 189.

24. Clark Pinnock, *Set Forth Your Case* (New Jersey: The Craig Press, 1968), p. 58.

5

Who Would Die for a Lie?

One area often overlooked in challenges to Christianity is the transformation of Jesus' apostles. Their changed lives provide solid testimony for the validity of his claims. Since the Christian faith is historical, to investigate it we must rely heavily upon testimony, both written and oral.

There are many definitions of "history," but the one I prefer is "a knowledge of the past based upon testimony." If someone says, "I don't believe that's a good definition," I ask, "Do you believe that Napoleon lived?" They almost always reply, "Yes." "Have you seen him?" I ask, and they confess they haven't. "How do you know, then?" Well, they are relying on testimony.

This definition of history has one inherent problem. The testimony must be reliable or the hearer will be misinformed. Christianity involves knowledge of the past based upon testimony, so now we must ask, "Were the original oral testimonies about Jesus trustworthy? Can they be trusted to have conveyed correctly what Jesus said and did?" I believe they can be.

I can trust the apostles' testimonies because, of those twelve men, eleven died martyrs' deaths on the basis of two things: the resurrection of Christ, and their belief in him as the Son of God. They were tortured and flogged, and they finally faced death by some of the cruelest methods then known:

1) Peter—crucified
2) Andrew—crucified
3) Matthew—the sword
4) John—natural
5) James, son of Alphaeus—crucified
6) Philip—crucified
7) Simon—crucified
8) Thaddaeus—killed by arrows
9) James, brother of Jesus—stoned
10) Thomas—spear thrust
11) Bartholomew—crucified
12) James, son of Zebedee—the sword

The response that is usually chorused back is this: "Why, a lot of people have died for a lie; so what does it prove?"

Yes, a lot of people have died for a lie, but they thought it was the truth. Now if the resurrection didn't take place [i.e., was false], the disciples knew it. I find no way to demonstrate that they could have been deceived. Therefore these eleven men not only died for a lie—here is the catch—but they knew it was a lie. It would be hard to find eleven people in history who died for a lie, knowing it was a lie.

We need to be cognizant of several factors in order to appreciate what they did. First, when the apostles wrote or spoke, they did so as eyewitnesses of the events they described.

Peter said: "For we did not follow cleverly devised tales when we made known to you the power and coming of our Lord Jesus Christ, but we were eyewitnesses of his majesty" (2 Peter 1:16). The apostles certainly knew the difference between myth or legend and reality.

John emphasized the eyewitness aspect of the Jews' knowledge: "What was from the beginning, what we have heard, what we have seen with our eyes, what we beheld and our hands handled, concerning the Word of life—and the life was manifested, and we have seen and bear witness and proclaim to you the eternal life, which was with the Father and was manifested to us—what we have seen and heard we proclaim to you also, that you also may have fellowship with us; and indeed our fellowship is with the Father, and with His Son Jesus Christ" (1 John 1:1-3).

Luke said: "Inasmuch as many have undertaken to compile an account of the things accomplished among us, just as those who from the beginning were eyewitnesses and servants of the Word have handed them down to us, it seemed fitting for me as well, having investigated everything carefully from the beginning, to write it out for you in consecutive order" (Luke 1:1-3).

Then in the book of Acts, Luke described the forty-day period after the resurrection when his followers closely observed him: "The first account I composed...about all that Jesus began to do and teach, until the day when He was taken up, after He had by the Holy Spirit given orders to the apostles whom He had chosen. To these He also presented Himself alive, after His suffering, by many convincing proofs, appearing to them over a period of forty days, and speaking of the things concerning the kingdom of God" (Acts 1:1-3).

John began the last portion of his Gospel by saying that there were "many other signs therefore Jesus also performed in the presence of the disciples, which are not written in this book" (John 20:30).

The main content of these eyewitness testimonies concerned the resurrection. The apostles were witnesses of his resurrected life:

Luke 24:48	Acts 3:15
John 15:27	Acts 4:33
Acts 1:8	Acts 5:32
Acts 2:24,32	Acts 10:39
Acts 10:41	1 John 1:2
Acts 13:31	Acts 22:15
1 Corinthians 15:4-9	Acts 23:11
1 Corinthians 15:15	Acts 26:16

Second, the apostles themselves had to be convinced that Jesus was raised from the dead. At first they hadn't believed. They went and hid (Mark 14:50). They didn't hesitate to express their doubts. Only after ample and convincing evidence did they believe. There was Thomas, who said he wouldn't believe that Christ was raised from the dead until he had put his finger in the nail prints. Thomas later died a martyr's death for Christ. Was he deceived? He bet his life he wasn't.

Then there was Peter. He denied Christ several times during his trial. Finally he deserted Jesus. But something happened to this coward. Just a short time after Christ's crucifixion and burial, Peter showed up in Jerusalem preaching boldly, at the threat of death, that Jesus was the Christ and had been resurrected. Finally Peter was crucified upside down. Was he deceived? What had happened to him? What had transformed him so dramatically into a bold lion for Jesus? Why was he willing to die for him? The only explanation I am satisfied with is 1 Corinthians 15:5—"and then He appeared to Cephas [Peter]" (John 1:42).

The classic example of a man convinced against his will was James, the brother of Jesus (Matthew 13:55; Mark 6:3). Although James wasn't one of the original twelve (Matthew 10:2-4), he was later recognized as an apostle (Galatians 1:19), as were Paul and Barnabas (Acts 14:14). When Jesus was alive, James didn't believe in his brother Jesus as the Son of God (John 7:5). He as well as his brothers and sisters may even have mocked him. "You want people to believe in you? Why don't you go up to Jerusalem and do your thing?" For James it must have been humiliating for Jesus to go around and bring ridicule to the family name by his wild claims ("I am the way, and the truth, and the life; no one comes to the Father, but through Me"—John 14:6; "I am the vine, you are the branches"—John 15:5; "I am the good shepherd...and My own know Me"—John 10:14). What would *you* think if your brother said such things?

But something happened to James. After Jesus was crucified and buried, James was preaching in Jerusalem. His message was that Jesus died for sins and was resurrected and is alive. Eventually James became one of the leaders of the Jerusalem church and wrote a book, the epistle of James. He began it by writing, "James, a servant of God and of the Lord Jesus Christ." His brother. Eventually James died a martyr's death by stoning at the hands of Ananias the high priest [Josephus]. Was James deceived? No, the only plausible explanation is 1 Corinthians 15:7—"then He appeared to James."

If the resurrection was a lie, the apostles knew it. Were they perpetuating a colossal hoax? That possibility is inconsistent with what we know about the moral quality of their lives. They personally condemned lying and stressed honesty. They encouraged people to know the truth. The historian Edward Gibbon in his famous work, *The History of the Decline and Fall of the Roman Empire,* gives the "purer but austere morality of the first Christians" as one of five reasons for the rapid success of Christianity. Michael Green, principal of St. John's College, Nottingham, observes that the resurrection "was the belief that turned heartbroken followers of a crucified rabbi into the courageous witnesses and martyrs of the early church. This was the one belief that separated the followers of Jesus from the Jews and turned them into the community of the resurrection. You could imprison them, flog them, kill them, but you could not make them deny their conviction that 'on the third day he rose again.' "[1]

Third, the bold conduct of the apostles immediately after they were convinced of the resurrection makes it unlikely that it all was a fraud. They became bold almost overnight. Peter who had denied Christ stood up even at the threat of death and proclaimed Jesus alive after the resurrection. The authorities arrested the followers of Christ and beat them, yet they soon would be back in the street speaking out about Jesus (Acts 5:40-42). Their friends noticed their buoyancy and their enemies noticed their courage. Nor did they preach in an obscure town, but in Jerusalem.

Jesus' followers couldn't have faced torture and death unless they were convinced of his resurrection. The unanimity of their message and course of conduct was amazing. The chances against any large group being in agreement is enormous, yet they all agreed on the truth of the resurrection. If they were deceivers, it's hard to explain why one of them didn't break down under pressure.

Pascal, the French philosopher, writes: "The allegation that the Apostles were imposters is quite absurd. Let us follow the charge to its logical conclusion: Let us picture those twelve men, meeting after the death of Jesus Christ, and entering into conspiracy to say that He has risen. That would have constituted an attack upon both the civil and the religious authorities. The heart of man is strangely given to fickleness and change; it is swayed by promises, tempted by material things. If any one of those men had yielded to temptations so alluring, or given way to the more compelling arguments of prison, torture, they would have all been lost."[2]

"How have they turned, almost overnight," asks Michael Green, "into the indomitable band of enthusiasts who braved opposition, cynicism, ridicule, hardship, prison, and death in three continents, as they preached everywhere Jesus and the resurrection?"[3]

An unknown writer descriptively narrates the changes that occurred in the lives of the apostles: "On the day of the crucifixion they were filled with sadness; on the first day of the week with gladness. At the crucifixion they were hopeless; on the first day of the week their hearts glowed with certainty and hope. When the message of the resurrection first came they were incredulous and hard to be convinced, but once they became assured they never doubted again. What could account for the astonishing change in these men in so short a time? The mere removal of the body from the grave could never have transformed their spirits and characters. Three days are not enough for a legend to spring up which would so affect them. Time is needed for a process of legendary growth. It is a psychological fact that demands a full explanation. Think of the character of the witnesses, men and women who gave the world the highest ethical teaching it has ever known, and who even on the testimony of their enemies lived it out in their lives. Think of the psychological absurdity of picturing a little band of defeated cowards cowering in an upper room one day and a few days later transformed into a company that no persecution could silence—and then attempting to attribute this dramatic change to nothing more convincing than a miserable fabrication they were trying to foist upon the world. That simply wouldn't make sense."

Kenneth Scott Latourette writes: "The effects of the resurrection and the coming of the Holy Spirit upon the disciples were...of major importance. From discouraged, disillusioned men and women who sadly looked back upon the days when they had hoped that Jesus 'was he who should redeem Israel,' they were made over into a company of enthusiastic witnesses."[4]

Paul Little asks: "Are these men, who helped transform the moral structure of society, consummate liars or deluded madmen? These alternatives are harder to believe than the fact of the Resurrection, and there is no shred of evidence to support them."[5]

The steadfastness of the apostles even to death cannot be explained away. According to the *Encyclopaedia Britannica,* Origen records that Peter was crucified head downward. Herbert Workman describes Peter's death: "Thus Peter, as our Lord had prophesied, was 'girt' by another, and 'carried' out to die along the Aurelian Way, to a place hard by the gardens of Nero on the Vatican hill, where so many of his brethren had already suffered a cruel death. At his own request he was crucified head downwards, as unworthy to suffer like his master."[6]

Harold Mattingly, in his history text, writes: "The apostles, St. Peter and St. Paul, sealed their witnesses with their blood."[7] Tertullian wrote that "no man would be willing to die unless he knew he had the truth."[8] Harvard law professor Simon Greenleaf, a man who lectured for years on how to break down a witness and determine whether or not a witness is lying, concludes: "The annals of military warfare afford scarcely an example of the like heroic constancy, patience, and unflinching courage. They had every possible motive to review carefully the grounds of their faith, and the evidences of the great facts and truths which they asserted."[9]

The apostles went through the test of death to substantiate the veracity of what they were proclaiming. I believe I can trust their testimony more than that of most people I meet today, people who aren't willing to walk across the street for what they believe, let alone die for it.

NOTES ON CHAPTER 5

1. Michael Green, "Editor's Preface" In George Eldon Ladd, *I Believe in the Resurrection of Jesus* (Grand Rapids: William B. Eerdmans Publishing Co., 1975).

2. Robert W. Gleason (Ed.), *The Essential Pascal,* Trans. by G.F. Pullen (New York: Mentor-Omega Books, 1966), p. 187.

3. Michael Green, *Man Alive!* (Downers Grove, Ill.: InterVarsity Press, 1968), pp. 23-24.

4. Kenneth Scott Latourette, *A History of Christianity* (New York: Harper and Brothers Publishers, 1937) Vol. I, p. 59.

5. Paul Little, *Know Why You Believe* (Wheaton, Ill: Scripture Press Publications, Inc., 1971), p. 63.

6. Herbert B. Workman, *The Martyrs of the Early Church* (London: Charles H. Kelly, 1913), pp. 18-19.

7. Harold Mattingly, *Roman Imperial Civilization* (London: Edward Arnold Publishers, Ltd., 1967), p. 226.

8. Gaston Foote, *The Transformation of the Twelve* (Nashville: Abingdon Press, 1958), p. 12.

9. Simon Greenleaf, *An Examination of the Testimony of the Four Evangelists by the Rules of Evidence Administered in the Courts of Justice* (Grand Rapids: Baker Book House, 1965. Reprint of 1874 edition. New York: J. Cockroft and Co.), p. 29.

6

What Good Is a Dead Messiah?

A lot of people have died for a good cause. Look at the student in San Diego who burned himself to death protesting against the Vietnam war. In the sixties many Buddhists burned themselves to death in order to bring world attention to Southeast Asia.

The problem with the apostles is that their good cause died on the cross. They believed Jesus to be the Messiah. They didn't think he could die. They were convinced that he was the one to set up the kingdom of God and to rule over the people of Israel.

In order to understand the apostles' relationship to Christ and to understand why the cross was so incomprehensible to them, you have to grasp the attitude about the Messiah at the time of Christ.

The life and teachings of Jesus were in tremendous conflict with the Jewish messianic speculation of that day. From childhood a Jew was taught that when the Messiah came, he would be a reigning, victorious, political leader. He would release the Jews from bondage and restore Israel to its rightful place. A suffering Messiah was "completely foreign to the Jewish conception of messiahship."[1]

E.F. Scott gives his account of the time of Christ: "...the period was one of intense excitement. The religious leaders found it almost impossible to restrain the ardour of the people, who were waiting everywhere for the appearance of the promised Deliverer. This mood of expectancy had no doubt been heightened by the events of recent history.

"For more than a generation past the Romans had been encroaching on Jewish freedom, and their measures of repression had stirred the spirit of patriotism to fiercer life. The dream of a miraculous deliverance, and of a Messianic king who would effect it, assumed a new meaning in that critical time; but in itself it was nothing new. Behind the ferment of which we have evidence in the Gospels, we can discern a long period of growing anticipation.

"To the people at large the Messiah remained what he had been to Isaiah and his contemporaries—the Son of David who would bring victory and prosperity to the Jewish nation. In the light of the Gospel references it can hardly be doubted that the popular conception of the Messiah was mainly national and political."[2]

Jewish scholar Joseph Klausner writes: "The Messiah became more and more not only a preeminent political ruler but also a man of preeminent moral qualities."[3]

Jacob Gartenhaus reflects the prevailing Jewish beliefs of the time of Christ: "The Jews awaited the Messiah as the one who would deliver them from Roman oppression...the messianic hope was basically for a national liberation."[4]

The *Jewish Encyclopaedia* states that the Jews "yearned for the promised deliverer of the house of David, who would free them from the yoke of the hated foreign usurper, would put an end to the impious Roman rule, and would establish His own reign of peace and justice in its place."[5]

At that time the Jews were taking refuge in the promised Messiah. The apostles held the same beliefs as the people around them. As Millar Burrows stated, "Jesus was so unlike what all Jews expected the son of David to be that His own disciples found it almost impossible to connect the idea of the Messiah with Him."[6] The grave communications by Jesus about being crucified were not at all welcomed by his disciples (Luke 9:22). There "seems to have been the hope," observes A.B. Bruce, "that He had taken too gloomy a view of the situation, and that His apprehensions would turn out groundless...a crucified Christ was a scandal and a contradiction to the apostles; quite as much as it continued to be to the majority of the Jewish people after the Lord had ascended to glory."[7]

Alfred Edersheim, once Grinfield Lecturer on the Septuagint at Oxford, was right in concluding that "the most unlike thing to Christ were His times."[8]

One can detect in the New Testament the apostles' attitude toward Christ: their expectation of a reigning Messiah. After Jesus told his disciples that he had to go to Jerusalem and suffer, James and John asked him to promise that in his kingdom they could sit on his right and left hands (Mark 10:32-38). What type of Messiah were they thinking of? A suffering, crucified Messiah? No, a political ruler. Jesus indicated that they misunderstood what he had to do; they didn't know what they were asking. When Jesus predicted his suffering and crucifixion, the twelve apostles couldn't figure out what he meant (Luke 18:31-34). Because of their background and training they believed they were in on a good thing. Then came Calvary. All hopes departed of Jesus being their Messiah. Discouraged, they returned to their homes. All those years wasted.

Dr. George Eldon Ladd, professor of New Testament at Fuller Theological Seminary, writes: "This is also why his disciples forsook him when he was taken captive. Their minds were so completely imbued with the idea of a conquering Messiah whose role it was to subdue his enemies that when they saw him broken and bleeding under the scourging, a helpless prisoner in the hands of Pilate, and when they saw him led away, nailed to a cross to die as a common criminal, all their messianic hopes for Jesus were shattered. It is a sound psychological fact that we hear only what we are prepared to hear. Jesus' predictions of his suffering and death fell on deaf ears. The disciples, in spite of his warnings, were unprepared for it..."[9]

But a few weeks after the crucifixion, in spite of their former doubts, the disciples were in Jerusalem proclaiming Jesus as Savior and Lord, the Messiah of the Jews. The only reasonable explanation that I can see of this change is 1 Corinthians 15:5—"He appeared... then to the twelve." What else could have caused the despondent disciples to go out and suffer and die for a crucified Messiah? He certainly must have "presented Himself alive, after His suffering, by many convincing proofs, appearing to them over a period of forty days" (Acts 1:3).

Yes, a lot of people have died for a good cause, but the good cause of the apostles died on the cross. Only the resurrection and resultant contact with Christ convinced his followers he was the Messiah. To this they testified not only with their lips and lives, but with their deaths.

NOTES ON CHAPTER 6

1. *Encyclopedia International,* 1972, Vol. 4, p. 407.
2. Ernest Findlay Scott, *Kingdom and the Messiah* (Edinburgh: T. & T. Clark, 1911), p. 55.
3. Joseph Klausner, *The Messianic Idea in Israel* (New York: The MacMillan Co., 1955), p. 23.
4. Jacob Gartenhaus, "The Jewish Conception of the Messiah," *Christianity Today,* March 13, 1970, pp. 8-10.

5. *The Jewish Encyclopaedia* (New York: Funk and Wagnalls Co., 1906), Vol. 8, p. 508.

6. Millar Burrows, *More Light on the Dead Sea Scrolls* (London: Secker & Warburg, 1958), p. 68.

7. A.B. Bruce, *The Training of the Twelve* (original 1894) (Grand Rapids: Kregel Publications, 1971), p. 177.

8. Alfred Edersheim, *Sketches of Jewish Social Life in the Days of Christ* (reprint edition; Grand Rapids: William B. Eerdmans Publishing Co., 1960), p. 29.

9. George Eldon Ladd, *I Believe in the Resurrection of Jesus* (Grand Rapids: William B. Eerdmans Publishing Co., 1975), p. 38.

7

Did You Hear What Happened to Saul?

Jack, a friend of mine who has spoken in many universities, was surprised one day when he arrived at a campus. He discovered that the students had arranged for him to have a public discussion that night with the "university atheist." His opponent was an eloquent philosophy professor who was extremely antagonistic to Christianity. Jack was to speak first. He discussed various proofs for the resurrection of Jesus, the conversion of the apostle Paul, and then gave his personal testimony about how Christ had changed his life when he was a university student.

When it was time for the professor to speak, he was very nervous. He couldn't refute the evidence for the resurrection, or Jack's personal testimony, so he turned to the subject of the Apostle Paul's radical conversion to Christianity. He used the line of argument that "people can often be so psychologically involved in what they're combating that they end up embracing it." At this point my friend smiled gently, and responded, "You'd better be careful, sir, or you're liable to become a Christian."

One of the most influential testimonies to Christianity was when Saul of Tarsus perhaps Christianity's most rabid antagonist, became the Apostle Paul. Saul was a Hebrew zealot, a religous leader. Being born in Tarsus gave him the opportunity to be exposed to the most advanced learning of his day. Tarsus was a university city known for its Stoic philosophers and culture. Strabo, the Greek geographer, praised Tarsus for being so interested in education and philosophy.[1a]

Paul, like his father, possessed Roman citizenship, a high privilege. He seemed to be well versed in Hellenistic culture and thought. He had great command of the Greek language and displayed dialectic skill. He quoted from less familiar poets and philosophers:

Acts 17:28—"For in him we live and move and exist [Epimenides], as even some of your own poets have said, 'For we also are His offspring' [Aratus, Cleanthes]";

1 Corinthians 15:33—"Do not be deceived: 'Bad company corrupts good morals' [Menander]";

Titus 1:12—"One of themselves, a prophet of their own, said, 'Cretans are always liars, evil beasts, lazy gluttons' [Epimenides]."

Paul's education was Jewish and took place under the strict doctrines of the Pharisees. At about age fourteen, he was sent to study under Gamaliel, one of the great rabbis of the time, the grandson of Hillel. Paul asserted that he was not only a Pharisee but the son of Pharisees (Acts 23:6). He could boast: "I was advancing in Judaism beyond many of my contemporaries among my countrymen, being more extremely zealous for my ancestral traditions" (Galatians 1:14).

If one is to understand Paul's conversion, it is necessary to see why he was so vehemently anti-Christian: the reason was his devotion to the Jewish law, which triggered his adamant discontent with Christ and the early church.

Paul's "offence with the Christian message was not," as Jacques Dupont writes, "with the affirmation of Jesus' messiahship [but]...with the attributing to Jesus of a saving role which robbed the law of all its value in the purpose of salvation...[Paul was] violently hostile to the Christian faith because of the importance which he attached to the law as a way of salvation."[2]

The Encyclopaedia Britannica states that the new sect of Judaism calling themselves Christians struck at the essence of Paul's Jewish training and rabbinic studies.[1b] To exterminate this sect became his passion (Galatians 1:13). So Paul began his pursuit to death of "the sect of the Nazarenes" (Acts 26:9-11). He literally "laid waste the church" (Acts 8:3). He set out for Damascus with documents authorizing him to seize the followers of Jesus and bring them back to face trial.

Then something happened to Paul. "Now Saul, still breathing threats and murder against the disciples of the Lord, went to the high priest, and asked for letters from him to the synagogues at Damascus, so that if he found any belonging to the Way, both men and women, he might bring them bound to Jerusalem. And it came about that as he journeyed, he was approaching Damascus, and suddenly a light from heaven flashed around him; and he fell to the ground, and heard a voice saying to him, 'Saul, Saul, why are you persecuting Me?' And he said, 'Who art Thou, Lord?' And He said, 'I am Jesus whom you are persecuting, but rise, and enter the city, and it shall be told you what you must do.' And the men who traveled with him stood speechless, hearing the voice, but seeing no one. And Saul got up from the ground, and though his eyes were open, he could see nothing; and leading him by the hand, they brought him into Damascus. And he was three days without sight, and neither ate nor drank.

"Now there was a certain disciple at Damascus, named Ananias; and the Lord said to him in a vision, 'Ananias.' And he said, 'Behold, here am I, Lord.' And the Lord said to him 'Arise and go to the street called Straight, and inquire at the house of Judas for a man from Tarsus named Saul, for behold, he is praying, and he has seen in a vision a man named Ananias come in and lay his hands on him, so that he might regain his sight" (Acts 9:1-12).

At this point one can see why Christians feared Paul. Ananias answered: " 'Lord, I have heard from many about this man, how much harm he did to Thy saints at Jerusalem; and here he has authority from the chief priests to bind all who call upon Thy name.' But the Lord said to him, 'Go, for he is a chosen instrument of Mine, to bear My name before the Gentiles and kings and the sons of Israel; for I will show him how much he must suffer for My name's sake.' And Ananias departed and entered the house, and after laying his hands on him said, 'Brother Saul, the Lord Jesus, who appeared to you on the road by which you were coming, has sent me so that you may regain your sight, and be filled with the Holy Spirit.' And immediately there fell from his eyes something like scales, and he regained his sight, and he arose and was baptized; and he took food and was strengthened" (Acts 9:13-19a). Paul said, "Have I not seen Jesus our Lord?" (1 Corinthians 9:1). He compared Christ's appearance to him with Christ's postresurrection appearances among the apostles. "And last of all...He appeared to me also" (1 Corinthians 15:8).

Not only did Paul see Jesus, but he saw him in an irresistible way. He didn't proclaim the gospel out of choice but from necessity. "For if I preach the gospel, I have nothing to boast of, for I am under compulsion" (1 Corinthians 9:16).

Notice that Paul's encounter with Jesus and subsequent conversion were sudden and unexpected. "A very bright light suddenly flashed from heaven all around me" (Acts 22:6). Paul had no idea

who this heavenly person could be. The announcement that it was
Jesus of Nazareth left him trembling and astonished.

We might not know all the details, chronology, or psychology
of what happened to Paul on the road to Damascus but we do know
this: it radically affected every area of his life.

First, Paul's character was drastically transformed. *The Encyclopaedia Britannica* decribes him before his conversion as an intol-
erant, bitter, persecuting, religious bigot—proud and temperamen-
tal. After his conversion he is pictured as patient, kind, enduring,
and self-sacrificing.[1c] Kenneth Scott Latourette says: "What inte-
grated Paul's life, however, and lifted this almost neurotic temtpera-
ment out of obscurity into enduring influence was a profound and
revolutionary religious experience."[3]

Second, Paul's relationship with the followers of Jesus was
transformed. "Now for several days he was with the disciples who
were at Damascus" (Acts 9:19). And when Paul went to the apostles,
he received the "right hand of fellowship."

Third, Paul's message was transformed. Though he still loved
his Jewish heritage, he had changed from a bitter antagonist to a determined protagonist of the Christian faith. "Immediately he began
to proclaim Jesus in the synagogues, saying, 'He is the Son of God'
(Acts 9:20). Paul's intellectual convictions had changed. His experience compelled him to acknowledge that Jesus was the Messiah, in
direct conflict with the Pharisees' messianic ideas. His new conception of Christ meant a total revolution in his thought.[4] Jacques Dupont acutely observes that after Paul "had passionately denied that a
crucified man could be the Messiah, he came to grant that Jesus was
indeed the Messiah, and, as a consequence, rethought all his messianic ideas."[2]

Also he could now understand that Christ's death on the cross,
which appeared to be a curse of God and a deplorable ending of
someone's life, was actually God through Christ reconciling the
world to himself. Paul came to understand that through the crucifixion Christ became a curse for us (Galatians 3:13) and was "made...
to be sin on our behalf" (2 Corinthians 5:21). Instead of a defeat, the
death of Christ was a great victory, being capped by the resurrection.
The cross was no longer a "stumbling block" but the essence of
God's messianic redemption. Paul's missionary preaching can be
summarized as "explaining and giving evidence that the Christ had
to suffer and rise again from the dead...'This Jesus whom I am proclaiming to you is the Christ,' " he said (Acts 17:3).

Fourth, Paul's mission was transformed. He was changed from
a Gentile-hater to a missionary to Gentiles. He was changed from a

Jewish zealot to an evangelist to Gentiles. As a Jew and Pharisee, Paul looked down upon the despised Gentile as someone inferior to God's chosen people. The Damascus experience changed him into a dedicated apostle, with his life's mission aimed toward helping the Gentile. Paul saw in the Christ who appeared to him the Savior for all people. Paul went from being an orthodox Pharisee whose mission was to preserve strict Judaism to being a propagator of that new radical sect called Christianity which he had so violently opposed. There was such a change in him that "all those hearing him continued to be amazed, and were saying 'Is this not he who in Jerusalem destroyed those who called on this [Jesus'] name, and who had come here for the purpose of bringing them bound before the chief priests?' " (Acts 9:21).

Historian Philip Schaff states: "The conversion of Paul marks not only a turning-point in his personal history, but also an important epoch in the history of the apostolic church, and consequently in the history of mankind. It was the most fruitful event since the miracle of Pentecost, and secured the universal victory of Christianity."[5]

During lunch at the University of Houston, I sat down next to a student. As we discussed Christianity he made the statement that there wasn't any historical evidence for Christianity or Christ. He was a history major and I noticed that one of his books was a Roman history textbook. He acknowledged that there was a chapter dealing with the Apostle Paul and Christianity. After reading the chapter, the student found it interesting that the section on Paul started by describing the life of Saul of Tarsus and ended with a description of the life of the Apostle Paul. In the next to the last paragraph the book observed that what happened in between was not clear. After I turned to the book of Acts and explained Christ's postresurrection appearance to Paul, this student saw that it was the most logical explanation of Paul's conversion. Later he also trusted Christ as his Savior.

Elias Andrews comments: "Many have found in the radical transformation of this 'Pharisee of the Pharisees' the most convincing evidence of the truth and the power of the religion to which he was converted, as well as the ultimate worth and place of the Person of Christ."[1d] Archibald MacBride, professor at the University of Aberdeen, writes of Paul: "Beside his achievements...the achievements of Alexander and Napoleon pale into insignificance."[6] Clement says that Paul "bore chains seven times; preached the gospel in the East and West; came to the limit of the West; and died a martyr under the rulers."[7]

Paul stated again and again that the living, resurrected Jesus had transformed his life. He was so convinced of Christ's resurrection from the dead that he, too, died a martyr's death for his beliefs.

Two professors at Oxford, Gilbert West and Lord Lyttleton, were determined to destroy the basis of the Christian faith. West was going to demonstrate the fallacy of the resurrection and Lyttleton was going to prove that Saul of Tarsus had never converted to Christianity. Both men came to the opposite conclusion and became ardent followers of Jesus. Lord Lyttleton writes: "The conversion and apostleship of Saint Paul alone, duly considered, was of itself a demonstration sufficient to prove Christianity to be a Divine Revelation."[8] He concludes that if Paul's twenty-five years of suffering and service for Christ were a reality, then his conversion was true, for everything he did began with that sudden change. And if his conversion was true, Jesus Christ rose from the dead, for everything Paul was and did he attributed to the sight of the risen Christ.

NOTES ON CHAPTER 7

1. *The Encyclopaedia Britannica,* William Benton, Publisher. (Chicago: Encyclopaedia Britannica, Inc., 1970), Vol. 17, *(a)* p. 469; *(b)* p. 476; *(c)* p. 473; *(d)* p. 469.
2. Jacques Dupont, "The Conversion of Paul, and Its Influence on His Understanding of Salvation by Faith," *Apostolic History and the Gospel.* Edited by W. Ward Gasque and Ralph P. Martin (Grand Rapids: Wm. B. Eerdmans Publishing Co., 1970), p. 177; p. 76.
3. Kenneth Scott Latourette, *A History of Christianity* (New York: Harper & Row, 1953), p. 76.
4. W.J. Sparrow-Simpson, *The Resurrection and the Christian Faith* (Grand Rapids: Zondervan Publishing House, 1968), pp. 185-186.
5. Philip Schaff, *History of the Christian Church,* Vol. I. Apostolic Christianity, A.D. 1-100 (Grand Rapids: Wm. B. Eerdmans Publishing Co., 1910), p. 296.
6. *Chambers's Encyclopedia* (London: Pergamon Press, 1966), Vol. 10, p. 516.
7. Philip Schaff, *History of the Apostolic Church* (New York: Charles Scribner, 1857), p. 340.
8. George Lyttleton, *The Conversion of St. Paul* (New York: American Tract Society, 1929), p. 467.

Can You Keep a Good Man Down?

A student at the University of Uruguay said to me, "Professor McDowell, why can't you refute Christianity?" I answered, "For a very simple reason. I'm unable to explain away an event in history—the resurrection of Jesus Christ."

After more than 700 hours of studying this subject and thoroughly investigating its foundation, I came to the conclusion that the resurrection of Jesus Christ is either one of the most wicked, vicious, heartless hoaxes ever foisted upon people, or it is the most important fact of history.

The resurrection issue takes the question "Is Christianity valid?" out of the realm of philosophy and makes it a question of history. Does Christianity have a historically acceptable basis? Is sufficient evidence available to warrant belief in the resurrection?

Some facts relevant to the resurrection are these: Jesus of Nazareth, a Jewish prophet who claimed to be the Christ prophesied in the Jewish Scriptures, was arrested, judged a political criminal, and crucified. Three days after his death and burial, some women who went to his tomb found the body gone. His disciples claimed that God had raised him from the dead and that he had appeared to them various times before ascending into heaven.

From this foundation, Christianity spread throughout the Roman Empire and has continued to exert great influence down through the centuries.

Did the resurrection actually happen?

JESUS' BURIAL

The body of Jesus, in accordance with Jewish burial customs, was wrapped in a linen cloth. About 100 pounds of aromatic spices, mixed together to form a gummy substance were applied to the wrappings of cloth about the body.[1]

After the body was placed in a solid rock tomb,[2] an extremely large stone (weighing approximately two tons) was rolled by means of levers against the entrance of the tomb.[3]

A Roman guard of strictly disciplined men was stationed to guard the tomb. Fear of punishment "produced flawless attention to duty, especially in the night watches."[4] This guard affixed on the tomb the Roman seal, a stamp of Roman power and authority.[5] The seal was meant to prevent vandalizing. Anyone trying to move the stone from the tomb's entrance would have broken the seal and thus incurred the wrath of Roman law.

But the tomb was empty.

THE EMPTY TOMB

The followers of Jesus said he had risen from the dead. They reported that he appeared to them during a period of forty days, showing himself to them by many "convincing proofs" (some versions say "infallible proofs").[6] Paul the apostle said that Jesus appeared to more than 500 of his followers at one time, the majority of whom were still alive and could confirm what Paul wrote.[7]

A.M. Ramsey writes: "I believe in the Resurrection, partly because a series of facts are unaccountable without it."[8] The empty tomb was "too notorious to be denied." Paul Althaus states that the resurrection "could not have been maintained in Jerusalem for a single day, for a single hour, if the emptiness of the tomb had not been established as a fact for all concerned."[9]

Paul L. Maier concludes: "If all the evidence is weighed carefully and fairly, it is indeed justifiable, according to the canons of historical research, to conclude that the tomb in which Jesus was buried was actually empty on the morning of the first Easter. And no shred of evidence has yet been discovered in literary sources, epigraphy, or archaeology that would disprove this statement."[10]

How can we explain the empty tomb? Can it possibly be accounted for by a natural cause?

Based on overwhelming historical evidence, Christians believe that Jesus was bodily resurrected in time and space by the supernatural power of God. The difficulties of belief may be great, but the problems inherent in unbelief present even greater difficulties.

The situation at the tomb after the resurrection is significant. The Roman seal was broken, which meant automatic crucifixion upside down for those who did it. The large stone was moved up and away from not just the entrance, but from the entire massive sepulchre, looking as if it had been picked up and carried away.[11] The guard unit had fled. Justin in his *Digest* 49.16 lists eighteen offenses for which a guard unit could be put to death. These included falling asleep or leaving one's position unguarded.

The women came and found the tomb empty; they panicked, and went back and told the men. Peter and John ran to the tomb. John got there first but he didn't enter it. He looked in and there were the grave clothes, caved in a little, but empty. The body of Christ had passed right through them into a new existence. Let's face it, that would make you quite a believer, at least for the moment.

The theories advanced to explain the resurrection from natural causes are weak; they actually help to build confidence in the truth of the resurrection.

THE WRONG TOMB?

A theory propounded by Kirsopp Lake assumes that the women who reported the body missing had mistakenly gone to the wrong tomb. If so, then the disciples who went to check up on the women's statement must also have gone to the wrong tomb. We can be certain, however, that the Jewish authorities, who had asked for that Roman guard to be stationed at the tomb to prevent the body from being stolen, wouldn't have been mistaken about the location. Nor would the Roman guards, for they were there.

If a wrong tomb were involved, the Jewish authorities would have lost no time in producing the body from the proper tomb, thus effectively quenching for all time any rumor of a resurrection.

Another attempt at explanation claims that the appearances of Jesus after the resurrection were either illusions or hallucinations. Unsupported by the psychological principles governing the appearances of hallucinations, this theory also does not coincide with the historical situation or with the mental state of the apostles.

So, where was the actual body, and why wasn't it produced?

SWOON THEORY

Popularized by Venturini several centuries ago and often quoted today, the swoon theory says that Jesus didn't really die; he merely fainted from exhaustion and loss of blood. Everyone thought him dead, but later he was resuscitated and the disciples thought it to be a resurrection.

The skeptic David Friedrich Strauss—himself no believer in the resurrection—gave the deathblow to any thought that Jesus revived from a swoon: "It is impossible that a being who had stolen half-dead out of the sepulchre, who crept about weak and ill, wanting medical treatment, who required bandaging, strengthening and indulgence, and who still at last yielded to his sufferings, could have given to the disciples the impression that he was a Conqueror over death and the grave, the Prince of Life, an impression which lay at the bottom of their future ministry. Such a resuscitation could only have weakened the impression which He had made upon them in life and in death, at the most could only have given it an elegiac voice, but could by no possibility have changed their sorrow into enthusiasm, have elevated their reverence into worship."[12]

THE BODY STOLEN?

Another theory maintains that the body was stolen by the disciples while the guard slept.[13] The depression and cowardice of the disciples provide a hardhitting argument against their suddenly becoming so brave and daring as to face a detachment of soldiers at the tomb and steal the body. They were in no mood to attempt anything like that.

J.N.D. Anderson has been dean of the faculty of law at the University of London, chairman of the department of Oriental law at the School of Oriental and African Studies, and director of the Institute of Advanced Legal Studies at the University of London. Commenting on the proposition that the disciples stole Christ's body, he says: "This would run totally contrary to all we know of them: their ethical teaching, the quality of their lives, their steadfastness, in suffering and persecution. Nor would it begin to explain their dramatic transformation from dejected and dispirited escapists into witnesses whom no opposition could muzzle."[14]

The theory that the Jewish or Roman authorities moved Christ's body is no more reasonable an explanation for the empty tomb than theft by the disciples. If the authorities had the body in their possession or knew where it was, why, when the disciples were preaching the resurrection in Jerusalem, didn't they explain that they had taken it?

If they had, why didn't they explain exactly where the body lay? Why didn't they recover the corpse, put it on a cart, and wheel it through the center of Jerusalem? Such an action would certainly have destroyed Christianity.

Dr. John Warwick Montgomery comments: "It passes the bounds of credibility that the early Christians could have manufactured such a tale and then preached it among those who might easily have refuted it simply by producing the body of Jesus."[15]

EVIDENCE FOR THE RESURRECTION

Professor Thomas Arnold, for fourteen years the headmaster of Rugby, author of a famous three-volume *History of Rome,* and appointed to the chair of modern history at Oxford, was well acquainted with the value of evidence in determining historical facts. He said: "I have been used for many years to study the histories of other times, and to examine and weigh the evidence of those who have written about them, and I know of no one fact in the history of mankind which is proved by better and fuller evidence of every sort, to the understanding of a fair inquirer, than the great sign which God has given us that Christ died and rose again from the dead."[16]

English scholar Brooke Foss Westcott said: "Taking all the evidence together, it is not too much to say that there is no historic incident better or more variously supported than the resurrection of Christ. Nothing but the antecedent assumption that it must be false could have suggested the idea of deficiency in the proof of it."[17]

Dr. Simon Greenleaf was one of the greatest legal minds we have had in this country. He was the famous Royall Professor of Law at Harvard University, and succeeded Justice Joseph Story as the Dane Professor of Law in the same university. H.W.H. Knotts in the *Dictionary of American Biography* says of him: "To the efforts of Story and Greenleaf is ascribed the rise of the Harvard Law School to its eminent position among the legal schools of the United States." While professor of law at Harvard, Greenleaf wrote a volume in which he examined the legal value of the apostles' testimony to the resurrection of Christ. He observed that it was impossible that the apostles "could have persisted in affirming the truths they had narrated, had not Jesus actually risen from the dead, and had they not known this fact as certainly as they knew any other fact."[18] Greenleaf concluded that the resurrection of Christ was one of the best supported events in history, according to the laws of legal evidence administered in courts of justice.

Another lawyer, Frank Morison, set out to refute the evidence for the resurrection. He thought that the life of Jesus was one of the most beautiful lives ever lived, but when it came to the resurrection he thought someone had come along and tacked a myth onto the story of Jesus. He planned to write an account of the last few days of Jesus. He would of course disregard the resurrection. He figured that an intelligent, rational approach to Jesus would completely discount his resurrection. However, upon approaching the facts with his legal background and training, he had to change his mind. He eventually wrote a best-seller, *Who Moved the Stone?* The first chapter was titled, "The Book That Refused to Be Written," and the rest of the chapters deal decisively with the evidence for Christ's resurrection.[19]

George Eldon Ladd concludes: "The only rational explanation for these historical facts is that God raised Jesus in bodily form."[20] A believer in Jesus Christ today can have complete confidence, as did the first Christians, that his faith is based, not on myth or legend, but on the solid historical fact of the risen Christ and the empty tomb.

Most important of all, the individual believer can experience the power of the risen Christ in his life today. First of all, he can know that his sins are forgiven.[21] Second, he can be assured of eternal life and his own resurrection from the grave.[22] Third, he can be released from a meaningless and empty life and be transformed into a new creature in Jesus Christ.[23]

What is your evaluation and decision? What do you think of the empty tomb? After examining the evidence from a judicial perspective, Lord Darling, former Chief Justice of England, concluded that "there exists such overwhelming evidence, positive and negative, factual and circumstantial, that no intelligent jury in the world could fail to bring in a verdict that the resurrection story is true."[24]

NOTES ON CHAPTER 8

1. John 19:39, 40.
2. Matthew 27:60.
3. Mark 16:4.
4. George Currie, *The Military Discipline of the Romans from the Founding of the City to the Close of the Republic*. An abstract of a thesis published under the auspices of the Graduate Council of Indiana University, 1928, pp. 41-43.
5. A.T. Robertson, *Word Pictures in the New Testament* (New York: R.R. Smith, Inc., 1931), p. 239.
6. Acts 1:3.
7. 1 Corinthians 15:3-8.

8. Arthur Michael Ramsey, *God, Christ and the World* (London: SCM Press, 1969), pp. 78-80.

9. Paul Althaus, *Die Wahrheit des kirchlichen Osterglaubens* (Gütersloh: C. Bertelsmann, 1941), pp. 22, 25ff.

10. *Independent, Press-Telegram,* Long Beach, Calif., Saturday, April 21, 1973, p. A-10.

11. Josh McDowell, *Evidence That Demands a Verdict* (San Bernardino, Calif: Campus Crusade for Christ International, 1973), p. 231.

12. David Frederick Strauss, *The Life of Jesus for the People* (London: Williams and Norgate, 1879, 2nd ed.), Vol. 1, p. 412.

13. Matthew 28:1-15.

14. J.N.D. Anderson, *Christianity: The Witness of History,* copyright Tyndale Press, 1970. Used by permission of InterVarsity Press, Downers Grove, Ill., p. 92.

15. John Warwick Montgomery, *History and Christianity* (Downers Grove, Ill.: InterVarsity Press, 1972), p. 78.

16. Thomas Arnold, *Christian Life—Its Hopes, Its Fears, and Its Close* (London: T. Fellowes, 1859, 6th ed.), p. 324.

17. Paul E. Little, *Know Why You Believe* (Wheaton: Scripture Press Publications, Inc., 1967), p. 70.

18. Simon Greeleaf, *An Examination of the Testimony of the Four Evangelists by the Rules of Evidence Administered in the Courts of Justice* (Grand Rapids: Baker Book House, 1965. Reprint of 1874 edition. New York: J. Cockroft and Co., 1874), p. 29.

19. Frank Morison, *Who Moved the Stone?* (London: Faber and Faber, 1930).

20. George Eldon Ladd, *I Believe in the Resurrection of Jesus* (Grand Rapids: William B. Eerdmans Publishing Co., 1975), p. 141.

21. 1 Corinthians 15:3.

22. 1 Corinthians 15:19-26.

23. John 10:10; 2 Corinthians 5:17.

24. Michael Green, *Man Alive* (Downers Grove, Ill.; InterVarsity Press, 1968), p. 54.

Will the Real Messiah Please Stand Up?

Jesus had various credentials to support his claims to being the Messiah, God's Son. In this chapter I want to deal with one credential often overlooked, one of the most profound: the fulfillment of prophecy in his life.

Over and over again Jesus appealed to the prophecies of the Old Testament to substantiate his claims as the Messiah. Galatians 4:4 says, "But when the fulness of the time came, God sent forth His Son, born of a woman, born under the Law." Here we have reference to the prophecies being fulfilled in Jesus Christ. "And beginning with Moses and with all the prophets he explained to them the things concerning Himself in all the Scriptures" (Luke 24:27). Jesus said to them, "These are My words which I spoke to you while I was still with you, that all things which are written about Me in the Law of Moses and the Prophets and the Psalms must be fulfilled" (v. 44). He said, "For if you believed Moses, you would believe Me; for he wrote of Me" (John 5:46). He said, "Abraham rejoiced to see My day" (John 8:56). The apostles, the New Testament writers, etc., constantly appealed to fulfilled prophecy to substantiate the claims of Jesus as the Son of God, the Savior, the Messiah. "But the things which God announced beforehand by the mouth of all the prophets, that His Christ should suffer, He has thus fulfilled" (Acts 3:18). "And according to Paul's custom, he went to them, and for three Sabbaths reasoned with them from the Scriptures [meaning the Old

Testament], explaining and giving evidence that the Christ had to suffer and rise again from the dead, and saying, 'This Jesus whom I am proclaiming to you is the Christ' " (Acts 17:2,3). "For I delivered to you as of first importance what I also received, that Christ died for our sins according to the Scriptures [in other words, Christ's death was prophesied in the Old Testament], and that He was buried, and that He was raised on the third day according to the Scriptures" (1 Corinthians 15:3,4).

In the Old Testament there are sixty major messianic prophecies and approximately 270 ramifications that were fulfilled in one person, Jesus Christ. It is helpful to look at all these predictions fulfilled in Christ as his "address." You've probably never realized how important the details of *your* name and address are—and yet these details set you apart from the four billion other people who also inhabit this planet.

AN ADDRESS IN HISTORY

With even greater detail, God wrote an "address" in history to single out his Son, the Messiah, the Savior of mankind, from anyone who has ever lived in history—past, present, and future. The specifics of this "address" can be found in the Old Testament, a document written over a period of 1,000 years which contains over 300 references to his coming. Using the science of probability, we find the chances of just forty-eight of these prophecies being fulfilled in one person to be only one in ten[157].

The task of matching up God's address with one man is further complicated by the fact that all the prophecies of the Messiah were made at least 400 years before he was to appear. Some might disagree and say that these prophecies were written down after the time of Christ and fabricated to coincide with his life. This might sound feasible until you realize that the Septuagint, the Greek translation of the Hebrew Old Testament, was translated around 150-200 B.C. This Greek translation shows that there was at least a two-hundred-year gap between the prophecies being recorded and their fulfillment in Christ.

Certainly God was writing an "address" in history that only the Messiah could fulfill. There have been approximately forty major claims by men to be the Jewish Messiah. But only one—Jesus Christ—appealed to fulfilled prophecy to substantiate his claims, and only his credentials back up those claims.

What were some of those details? And what events had to precede and coincide with the appearance of God's Son?

To begin, we need to go way back to Genesis 3:15. Here we have the first messianic prophecy. In all of Scripture, only one Man was "born of the seed of a woman"—all others are born of the seed of a man. Here is one who will come into the world and undo the works of Satan ("bruise his head").

In Genesis 9 and 10 God narrowed the "address" down further. Noah had three sons, Shem, Japheth, and Ham. Today all of the nations of the world can be traced back to these three men. But in this statement, God effectively eliminated two-thirds of them from the line of Messiahship. The Messiah will come through the lineage of Shem.

Then, continuing on down to the year 2000 B.C., we find God calling a man named Abraham out of Ur of the Chaldees. With Abraham, God became still more specific, stating that the Messiah will be one of his descendants.[1] All the families of the earth will be blessed through Abraham. When Abraham had two sons, Isaac and Ishmael, many of Abraham's descendants were eliminated when God selected his second son, Isaac.[2]

Isaac had two sons, Jacob and Esau, and then God chose the line of Jacob.[3] Jacob had twelve sons, out of whom developed the twelve tribes of Israel. Then God singled out the tribe of Judah for Messiahship and eliminated $11/12$ths of the Israelite tribes. And of all the family lines within Judah's tribe, the line of Jesse was the divine choice.[4] One can see the probability building.

Jesse had eight children and in 2 Samuel 7:12-16 and Jeremiah 23:5 God eliminated $7/8$ths of Jesse's family line: we read that God's Man will not only be of the seed of a woman, the lineage of Shem, the race of the Jews, the line of Isaac, the line of Jacob, the tribe of Judah, but that he will also be of the house of David.

A prophecy dating 1012 B.C.[5] also predicts that this Man's hands and feet will be pierced (i.e., he will be crucified). This description was written 800 years before crucifixion was put into effect by the Romans.

Isaiah 7:14 adds that he will be born of a virgin: a natural birth of unnatural conception, a criterion beyond human planning and control. Several prophecies recorded in Isaiah and the Psalms[6] describe the social climate and response that God's man will encounter: his own people, the Jews, will reject him and the Gentiles will believe in him. There will be a forerunner for him (Isaiah 40:3; Malachi 3:1), a voice in the wilderness, one preparing the way before the Lord, a John the Baptist.

THIRTY PIECES OF SILVER

Notice, too, the seven ramifications of a prophecy[7] that narrows the drama down even further. Here God indicates that the Messiah will (1) be betrayed, (2) by a friend, (3) for thirty pieces, (4) of silver, and that it will be (5) cast on the floor, (6) of the temple, and (7) used to buy a potter's field.

In Micah 5:2 God eliminated all the cities of the world and selected Bethlehem, with less than 1,000 people, as the Messiah's birthplace.

Then through a series of prophecies he even defined the time sequence that would set his Man apart. For example, Malachi 3:1 and four other Old Testament verses[8] require the Messiah to come while the temple of Jerusalem is still standing. This is of great significance when we realize that the temple was destroyed in A.D. 70 and has not since been rebuilt.

The precise lineage; the place, time, and manner of birth; people's reactions, the betrayal; the manner of death. These are just a fragment of the hundreds of details that made up the "address" to identify God's Son, the Messiah, the Savior of the world.

OBJECTION: SUCH FULFILLED PROPHECY WAS COINCIDENTAL

"Why, you could find some of these prophecies fulfilled in Kennedy, King, Nasser, etc.," replies a critic.

Yes, one could possibly find one or two prophecies fulfilled in other men, but not all sixty major prophecies and 270 ramifications. In fact, if you can find someone, other than Jesus, either living or dead, who can fulfill only half of the predictions concerning Messiah which are given in *Messiah in Both Testaments* by Fred John Meldau, the Christian Victory Publishing Company of Denver is ready to give you a $1,000 reward.

H. Harold Hartzler, of the American Scientific Affiliation, in the foreword of a book by Peter W. Stoner writes: "The manuscript for *Science Speaks* has been carefully reviewed by a committee of the American Scientific Affiliation members and by the Executive Council of the same group and has been found, in general, to be dependable and accurate in regard to the scientific material presented. The mathematical analysis included is based upon principles of probability which are thoroughly sound, and Professor Stoner has applied these principles in a proper and convincing way."[9]

The following probabilities are taken from that book to show that coincidence is ruled out by the science of probability. Stoner says that by using the modern science of probability in reference to eight prophecies, "we find that the chance that any man might have lived down to the present time and fulfilled all eight prophecies is 1 in 10^{17}." That would be 1 in 100,000,000,000,000,000. In order to help us comprehend this staggering probability, Stoner illustrates it by supposing that "we take 10^{17} silver dollars and lay them on the face of Texas. They will cover all of the state two feet deep. Now mark one of these silver dollars and stir the whole mass thoroughly, all over the state. Blindfold a man and tell him that he can travel as far as he wishes, but he must pick up one silver dollar and say that this is the right one. What chance would he have of getting the right one? Just the same chance that the prophets would have had of writing these eight prophecies and having them all come true in any one man, from their day to the present time, providing they wrote them in their own wisdom.

"Now these prophecies were either given by inspiration of God or the prophets just wrote them as they thought they should be. In such a case the prophets had just one chance in 10^{17} of having them come true in any man, but they all came true in Christ.

"This means that the fulfillment of these eight prophecies alone proves that God inspired the writing of those prophecies to a definiteness which lacks only one chance in 10^{17} of being absolute."[9]

ANOTHER OBJECTION

Another objection is that Jesus deliberately attempted to fulfill the Jewish prophecies. This objection seems plausible until we realize that many of the details of the Messiah's coming were totally beyond human control. For example, the place of birth. I can just hear Jesus in Mary's womb as she rode on the donkey: "Mom, we won't make it..." When Herod asked the chief priests and scribes, "Where is the Christ to be born?" they said, "In Bethlehem of Judea, for so it has been written by the prophet" (Matthew 2:5). The time of his coming. The manner of his birth. Betrayal by Judas and the betrayal price. The manner of his death. The people's reaction, the mocking and spitting, the staring. The casting of dice for his clothes. The non-tearing of his garment, etc. Half the prophecies are beyond his fulfillment. He couldn't work it out to be born of the seed of the woman, the lineage of Shem, the descendants of Abraham, etc. No wonder Jesus and the apostles appealed to fulfilled prophecy to substantiate his claim.

Why did God go to all this trouble? I believe he wanted Jesus Christ to have all the credentials he needed when he came into the world. Yet the most exciting thing about Jesus Christ is that he came to change lives. He alone proved correct the hundreds of Old Testament prophecies that described his coming. And he alone can fulfill the greatest prophecy of all for those who will accept it—the promise of new life: "I will give you a new heart and put a new spirit within you...Therefore if any man is in Christ, he is a new creature; the old things passed away; behold, new things have come."[10]

NOTES ON CHAPTER 9

1. Genesis 12; 17; 22.
2. Genesis 17; 21.
3. Genesis 28; 35:10-12; Numbers 24:17.
4. Isaiah 11:1-5.
5. Psalm 22:6-18; Zechariah 12:10; compare Galatians 3:13.
6. Isaiah 8:14; 28:16; 49:6; 50:6; 52:53; 60:3; Psalm 22:7,8; 118:22.
7. Zechariah 11:11-13; Psalm 41; compare Jeremiah 32:6-15 and Matthew 27:3-10.
8. Psalm 118:26; Daniel 9:26; Zechariah 11:13; Haggai 2:7-9. For a more complete discussion of the Daniel 9 prophecy, see pp. 178-181 of my book *Evidence That Demands a Verdict*.
9. Peter W. Stoner, and Robert C. Newman, *Science Speaks* (Chicago: Moody Press, 1976), pp. 106-112.
10. Ezekiel 36:25-27; 2 Corinthians 5:17.

10
Isn't There Some Other Way?

Recently at the University of Texas a graduate student approached me and asked, "Why is Jesus the only way to a relationship with God?" I had shown that Jesus claimed to be the only way to God, that the testimony of the Scriptures and the apostles was reliable, and that there was sufficient evidence to warrant faith in Jesus as Savior and Lord. Yet he had the question, "Why Jesus? Isn't there some other way to a relationship with God? What about Buddha? Mohammed? Can't an individual simply live a good life? If God is such a loving God, then wouldn't he accept all people just the way they are?"

A businessman said to me, "Evidently you have proven that Jesus Christ is the Son of God. Aren't there other ways also to a relationship with God apart from Jesus?"

The above comments are indicative of many people's questions today about why one has to trust Jesus as Savior and Lord in order to have a relationship with God and experience the forgiveness of sin. I answered the student by saying that many people don't understand the nature of God. Usually the question is "How can a loving God allow a sinful individual to go to hell?" I would ask, "How can a holy, just, righteous God allow a sinful individual into his presence?" A misunderstanding of the basic nature and character of God has been the cause of so many theological and ethical problems. Most people understand God to be a loving God and they don't go any further. The problem is that God is not only a God of love. He is also a righteous, just, and holy God.

We basically know God through his attributes. An attribute is not a part of God. I used to think that if I took all the attributes of God—holiness, love, justice, righteousness—and added them up, the sum total would equal God. Well, that's not true. An attribute isn't something that is a part of God but something that is true of God. For example, when we say God is love, we don't mean that a part of God is love, but that love is something that is true of God. When God loves he is simply being himself.

Here is a problem that developed as a result of humanity entering into sin. God in eternity past decided to create man and woman. Basically I believe that the Bible indicates he created man and woman in order to share his love and glory with them. But when Adam and Eve rebelled and went their own individual ways, sin entered the human race. At that point individuals became sinful or separated from God. This is the "predicament" that God found himself in. He created men and women to share his glory with them, yet they spurned his counsel and command and chose to sin. And so he approached them with his love to save them. But because he is not only a loving God, but a holy, just, righteous God, his very nature would destroy any sinful individual. The Bible says, "For the wages of sin is death." So, you might say, God had a problem.

Within the Godhead—God the Father, God the Son, and God the Holy Spirit—a decision was made. Jesus, God the Son, would take upon himself human flesh. He would become the God-man. This is described in John 1 where it says that the Word became flesh and tabernacled or dwelt among us. And also in Philippians 2 where it says that Christ Jesus emptied himself and took on the form of a man.

Jesus was the God-man. He was just as much man as if he had never been God and just as much God as if he had never been man. By his own choice he lived a sinless life, wholly obeying the Father. The biblical declaration that "the wages of sin is death" did not apply to him. Because he was not only finite man but infinite God, he had the infinite capacity to take upon himself the sins of the world. When he went to the cross almost 2000 years ago, a holy, just righteous God poured out his wrath upon his Son. And when Jesus said, "It is finished," the just righteous nature of God was satisfied. You could say that at that point God was "set free" to deal with humanity in love without having to destroy a sinful individual, because through Jesus' death on the cross, God's righteous nature was satisfied.

Often I ask people the question, "For whom did Jesus die?" and usually they reply, "For me" or "For the world." And I'll say, "Yes, that's right, but for whom else did Jesus die?" and usually they'll say, "Why, I don't know." I reply, "For God the Father." You see, Christ not only died for us but he also died for the Father. This is described in Romans 3 where it talks about propitiation. Propitiation basically means satisfaction of a requirement. And when Jesus died on the cross, he not only died for us but he died to meet the holy and just requirements of the basic nature of God.

An incident that took place several years ago in California illuminates what Jesus did on the cross in order to solve the problem God had in dealing with the sin of humanity. A young woman was picked up for speeding. She was ticketed and taken before the judge. The judge read off the citation and said, "Guilty or not guilty?" The woman replied, "Guilty." The judge brought down the gavel and fined her $100 or ten days. Then an amazing thing took place. The judge stood up, took off his robe, walked down around in front, took out his billfold, and paid the fine. What's the explanation of this? The judge was her father. He loved his daughter, yet he was a just judge. His daughter had broken the law and he couldn't simply say to her, "Because I love you so much, I forgive you. You may leave." If he had done that, he wouldn't have been a righteous judge. He wouldn't have upheld the law. But he loved his daughter so much that he was willing to take off his judicial robe and come down in front and represent her as her father and pay the fine.

This illustration pictures to some extent what God did for us through Jesus Christ. We sinned. The Bible says, "The wages of sin is death." No matter how much he loved us, God had to bring down the gavel and say *death,* because he is a righteous and just God. And yet, being a loving God, he loved us so much that he was willing to come down off the throne in the form of the man Christ Jesus and pay the price for us, which was Christ's death on the cross.

At this point many people ask the question, "Why couldn't God just forgive?" An executive of a large corporation said, "My employees often do something, break something, and I just forgive them." Then he added, "Are you trying to tell me I can do something that God can't do?" People fail to realize that wherever there is forgiveness there's a payment. For example, let's say my daughter breaks a lamp in my home. I'm a loving and forgiving father, so I put her on my lap, and I hug her and I say, "Don't cry, honey. Daddy loves you and forgives you." Now usually the person I tell that story to says, "Well, that's what God ought to do." Then I ask the question, "Who pays for the lamp?" The fact is, *I* do. There's always a price in forgiveness. Let's say somebody insults you in front of others and later you graciously say, "I forgive you." Who bears the price of the insult? You do.

This is what God has done. God has said, "I forgive you." But he was willing to pay the price himself through the cross.

11

He Changed My Life

Jesus Christ is alive. The fact that I'm alive and doing the things I do is evidence that Jesus Christ is raised from the dead.

Thomas Aquinas wrote: "There is within every soul a thirst for happiness and meaning." As a teen-ager I wanted to be happy. There's nothing wrong with that. I wanted to be one of the happiest individuals in the entire world. I also wanted meaning in life. I wanted answers to questions. "Who am I?" "Why in the world am I here?" "Where am I going?"

More than that, I wanted to be free. I wanted to be one of the freest individuals in the whole world. Freedom to me is not going out and doing what you want to do. Anyone can do that, and lots of people are doing it. Freedom is "to have the power to do what you know you ought to do." Most people know what they ought to do but they don't have the power to do it. They're in bondage.

So I started looking for answers. It seems that almost everyone is into some sort of religion, so I did the obvious thing and took off for church. I must have found the wrong church though. Some of you know what I'm talking about: I felt worse inside than I did outside. I went in the morning, I went in the afternoon, and I went in the evening.

I'm always very practical, and when something doesn't work, I chuck it. I chucked religion. The only thing I ever got out of religion was the twenty-five cents I put in the offering and the thirty-five cents I took out for a milkshake. And that's about all many people ever gain from "religion."

I began to wonder if prestige was the answer. Being a leader, accepting some cause, giving yourself to it, and "being known" might do it. In the first university I attended, the student leaders held the purse strings and threw their weight around. So I ran for freshman class president and got elected. It was neat knowing everyone on campus, having everyone say, "Hi, Josh," making the decisions, spending the university's money, the students' money, to get speakers I wanted. It was great but it wore off like everything else I had tried. I would wake up Monday morning, usually with a headache because of the night before, and my attitude was, "Well, here goes another five days." I endured Monday through Friday. Happiness revolved around three nights a week: Friday, Saturday, and Sunday. Then the vicious cycle began all over again.

Oh, I fooled them in the university. They thought I was one of the happiest-go-lucky guys around. During the political campaigns we used the phrase, "Happiness is Josh." I threw more parties with student money than anyone else did, but they never realized my happiness was like so many other people's. It depended on my own circumstances. If things were going great for me, I was great. When things would go lousy, I was lousy.

I was like a boat out in the ocean being tossed back and forth by the waves, the circumstances. There is a biblical term to describe that type of living: hell. But I couldn't find anyone living any other way and I couldn't find anyone who could tell me how to live differently or give me the strength to do it. I had everyone telling me what I ought to do but none of them could give me the power to do it. I began to be frustrated.

I suspect that few people in the universities and colleges of this country were more sincere in trying to find meaning, truth, and purpose to life than I was. I hadn't found it yet, but I didn't realize that at first. In and around the university I noticed a small group of people: eight students and two faculty members, and there was something different about their lives. They seemed to know why they believed what they believed. I like to be around people like that. I don't care if they don't agree with *me*. Some of my closest friends are opposed to some things I believe, but I admire a man or woman with conviction. (I don't meet many, but I admire them when I meet them.) That's why I sometimes feel more at home with some radical leaders than I do with many Christians. Some of the Christians I meet are so wishy-washy that I wonder if maybe 50 percent of them are masquerading as Christians. But the people in this small group seemed to know where they were going. That's unusual among university students.

The people I began to notice didn't just *talk* about love. They got involved. They seemed to be riding above the circumstances of university life. It appeared that everybody else was under a pile. One important thing I noticed was that they seemed to have a happiness, a state of mind not dependent on circumstances. They appeared to possess an inner, constant source of joy. They were disgustingly happy. They had something I didn't have.

Like the average student, when somebody had something I didn't have, I wanted it. That's why they have to lock up bicycles in colleges. If education were really the answer, the university would probably be the most morally upright society in existence. But it's not. So, I decided to make friends with these intriguing people.

Two weeks after that decision we were all sitting around a table in the student union, six students and two faculty members. The conversation started to get around to God. If you're an insecure person and a conversation centers on God, you tend to put on a big front. Every campus or community has a big mouth, a guy who says, "Uh...Christianity, ha, ha. That's for the weaklings, it's not intellectual." (Usually, the bigger the mouth, the bigger the vacuum.)

They were bothering me, so finally I looked over at one of the students, a good-looking woman (I used to think all Christians were ugly); and I leaned back in my chair because I didn't want the others to think I was interested, and I said, "Tell me, what changed your lives? Why are your lives so different from the other students, the leaders on campus, the professors? Why?"

That young woman must have had a lot of conviction. She looked me straight in the eye, no smile, and said two words I never thought I'd hear as part of a solution in a university. She said, "Jesus Christ." I said, "Oh, for God's sake, don't give me that garbage. I'm fed up with religion; I'm fed up with the church; I'm fed up with the Bible. Don't give me that garbage about religion." She shot back, "Mister, I didn't say religion, I said Jesus Christ." She pointed out something I'd never known before. Christianity is not a religion. Religion is humans trying to work their way to God through good works. Christianity is God coming to men and women through Jesus Christ offering them a relationship with himself.

There are probably more people in universities with misconceptions about Christianity than anywhere else in the world. Recently I met a teaching assistant who remarked in a graduate seminar that "anyone who walks into a church becomes a Christian." I replied, "Does walking into a garage make you a car?" There is no correlation. A Christian is somebody who puts his trust in Christ.

My new friends challenged me intellectually to examine the claims that Jesus Christ is God's Son; that taking on human flesh, he lived among real men and women and died on the cross for the sins of mankind, that he was buried and he arose three days later and could change a person's life in the twentieth century.

I thought this was a farce. In fact, I thought most Christians were walking idiots. I'd met some. I used to wait for a Christian to speak up in the classroom so I could tear him or her up one side and down the other, and beat the insecure professor to the punch. I imagined that if a Christian had a brain cell, it would die of loneliness. I didn't know any better.

But these people challenged me over and over. Finally, I accepted their challenge, but I did it out of pride, to refute them. But I didn't know there were facts. I didn't know there was evidence that a person could evaluate.

Finally, my mind came to the conclusion that Jesus Christ must have been who he claimed to be. In fact, the background of my first two books was my setting out to refute Christianity. When I couldn't, I ended up becoming a Christian. I have now spent thirteen years documenting why I believe that faith in Jesus Christ is intellectually feasible.

At that time, though, I had quite a problem. My mind told me all this was true but my will was pulling me in another direction. I discovered that becoming a Christian was rather ego-shattering. Jesus Christ made a direct challenge to my will to trust him. Let me paraphrase him. "Look! I have been standing at the door and I am constantly knocking. If anyone hears me calling him and opens the door, I will come in" (Revelation 3:20). I didn't care if he did walk on water or turn water into wine. I didn't want any party pooper around. I couldn't think of a faster way to ruin a good time. So here was my mind telling me Christianity was true and my will was somewhere else.

Every time I was around those enthusiastic Christians, the conflict would begin. If you've ever been around happy people when you're miserable, you understand how they can bug you. They would be so happy and I would be so miserable that I'd literally get up and run right out of the student union. It came to the point where I'd go to bed at ten at night and I wouldn't get to sleep until four in the morning. I knew I had to get it off my mind before I went out of my mind! I was always open-minded, but not so open-minded that my brains would fall out.

But since I was open-minded, on December 19, 1959, at 8:30 P.M. during my second year at the university, I became a Christian.

Somebody asked me, "How do you know?" I said, "Look, I was there. It's changed my life." That night I prayed. I prayed four things to establish a relationship with the resurrected, living Christ which has since transformed my life.

First, I said, "Lord Jesus, thank you for dying on the cross for me." Second, I said, "I confess those things in my life that aren't pleasing to you and ask you to forgive me and cleanse me." (The Bible says, "Though your sins be as scarlet they shall be as white as snow.") Third, I said, "Right now, in the best way I know how, I open the door of my heart and life and trust you as my Savior and Lord. Take over the control of my life. Change me from the inside out. Make me the type of person you created me to be.". The last thing I prayed was "Thank you for coming into my life by faith." It was a faith based not upon ignorance but upon evidence and the facts of history and God's Word.

I'm sure you've heard various religious people talking about their "bolt of lightning." Well, after I prayed, nothing happened. I mean nothing. And I still haven't sprouted wings. In fact, after I made that decision, I felt worse. I literally felt I was going to vomit. I felt sick deep down. "Oh no, what'd you get sucked into now?" I wondered. I really felt I'd gone off the deep end (and I'm sure some people think I did!).

I can tell you one thing: in six months to a year-and-a-half I found out that I hadn't gone off the deep end. My life *was* changed. I was in a debate with the head of the history department at a mid-western university and I said my life had been changed, and he interrupted me with "McDowell, are you trying to tell us that God really changed your life in the twentieth century? What areas?" After forty-five minutes he said, "Okay, that's enough."

One area I told him about was my restlessness. I always had to be occupied. I had to be over at my girl's place or somewhere else in a rap session. I'd walk across the campus and my mind was like a whirlwind with conflicts bouncing around the walls. I'd sit down and try to study or cogitate and I couldn't. But a few months after I made that decision for Christ, a kind of mental peace developed. Don't misunderstand. I'm not talking about the absence of conflict. What I found in this relationship with Jesus wasn't so much the absence of conflict but the ability to cope with it. I wouldn't trade that for anything in the world.

Another area that started to change was my bad temper. I used to blow my stack if somebody just looked at me cross-eyed. I still have the scars from almost killing a man my first year in the university. My temper was such a part of me that I didn't consciously seek to change it. I arrived at the crisis of losing my temper only to find it was gone! Only once in fourteen years have I lost my temper—and when I blew it that time, I made up for about six years!

There's another area of which I'm not proud. But I mention it because a lot of people need to have the same change in their lives, and I found the source of change: a relationship with the resurrected, living Christ. That area is hatred. I had a lot of hatred in my life. It wasn't something outwardly manifested, but there was a kind of inward grinding. I was ticked off with people, with things, with issues. Like so many other people, I was insecure. Every time I met someone different from me, he became a threat to me.

But I hated one man more than anyone else in the world. My father. I hated his guts. To me he was the town alcoholic. If you're from a small town and one of your parents is an alcoholic, you know what I'm talking about. Everybody knows. My friends would come to high school and make jokes about my father being downtown. They didn't think it bothered me. I was like other people, laughing on the outside, but let me tell you, I was crying on the inside. I'd go out in the barn and see my mother beaten so badly she couldn't get up, lying in the manure behind the cows. When we had friends over, I would take my father out, tie him up in the barn, and park the car up around the silo. We would tell our friends he'd had to go somewhere. I don't think anyone could have hated anyone more than I hated my father.

After I made that decision for Christ—maybe five months later—a love from God through Jesus Christ entered my life and was so strong it took that hatred and turned it upside down. I was able to look my father squarely in the eyes and say, "Dad, I love you." And I really meant it. After some of the things I'd done, that shook him up.

When I transferred to a private university I was in a serious car accident. My neck in traction, I was taken home. I'll never forget my father coming into my room. He asked me, "Son, how can you love a father like me?" I said, "Dad, six months ago I despised you." Then I shared with him my conclusions about Jesus Christ: "Dad, I let Christ come into my life. I can't explain it completely but as a result of that relationship I've found the capacity to love and accept not only you but other people just the way they are."

Forty-five minutes later one of the greatest thrills of my life occurred. Somebody in my own family, someone who knew me so well I couldn't pull the wool over his eyes, said to me, "Son, if God can do in my life what I've seen him do in yours, then I want to give him the opportunity." Right there my father prayed with me and trusted Christ.

Usually the changes take place over several days, weeks, or months, even a year. My life was changed in about six months to a year-and-a-half. The life of my father was changed right before my eyes. It was as if somebody reached down and turned on a light bulb. I've never seen such a rapid change before or since. My father touched whiskey only once after that. He got it as far as his lips and that was it. I've come to one conclusion. A relationship with Jesus Christ changes lives.

You can laugh at Christianity, you can mock and ridicule it. But it works. It changes lives. If you trust Christ, start watching your attitudes and actions, because Jesus Christ is in the business of changing lives.

But Christianity is not something you shove down somebody's throat or force on someone. You've got your life to live and I've got mine. All I can do is tell you what I've learned. After that, it's your decision.

Perhaps the prayer I prayed will help you: "Lord Jesus, I need you. Thank you for dying on the cross for me. Forgive me and cleanse me. Right this moment I trust you as Savior and Lord. Make me the type of person you created me to be. In Christ's name. Amen."

Portions of a dramatic
58-minute motion picture
"More Than A Carpenter"
are adapted from this paperback
by Josh McDowell.
For further information
about showing this film
write to:

Outreach Films
P.O. Box 1608
Burbank, CA 91507

Contents

Foreword

We are living in a disordered age. Most people, including Christians, are confused. They are bombarded by multitudes of voices and no two of them are in agreement; they are all saying different things. Which voice are we to believe or depend on? It's like going through a cafeteria line--you only go through once, you can't back up, and of the thousand things to choose from you must select one. Which will it be?

This brief book you are about to read has to do with Jesus. It says that you should choose Him. But which Jesus should you choose? And where do you go to find out about who Jesus is, where He came from, why He is here, what He did, where He is now, and when you will see Him? Thousands of books have been written about Jesus. Which of these books should I read?

The purpose of this work is to say rather dogmatically that the only true book you can trust that will tell you all you want to know about Jesus is the Bible. The Bible is the incomparable Book. It is the Word of God. Its author is God, who worked through chosen vessels to give us a Book we can trust in all of its parts. This Bible is the touchstone against which I can measure the words and opinions, as well as the works, of all men. Its main purpose is to bring us face to face with Jesus. He, along with His Father, and the Holy Spirit, are the major persons revealed and made known to us in this Book.

In writing about this Book, the Bible, I have sought to present the claims about the Bible as simply as possible. I have tried to write for lay people who have not studied in theological seminaries. I have kept the book brief, which means that many things have had to be left unsaid. I trust the readers will go on from here to read other better and more comprehensive works--so long as the Bible itself is read, studied, and pondered above all other works.

The chapter on the historical-critical method may present the most difficulties. It can be skimmed over on the first reading, but it is a very important chapter. The historical-critical method is perhaps the Bible's greatest enemy today. The historic Christian faith, theological orthodoxy, if you please, and the historical-critical methodology are antithetical. There is no way they can be reconciled. The victory of one means the defeat of the other.

The chief purpose of what you are about to read is to tell you plainly that the Scripture and the Word of God are one and the same; and that Scripture in all of its parts is trustworthy, or free from error, or infallible, or inerrant--for they all mean the same thing.

May God be pleased to use these words by His Spirit to bring to the hearts of every reader the assurance that God, the Author of Scripture, has spoken—and He has not stuttered in His speech.

I wish to thank the Zondervan Publishing House for permission to use a few small parts from a previous book of mine, *The Battle for the Bible.* And I wish to express my deep appreciation to the Concordia Publishing House for translating and printing *The End of the Historical-Critical Method* by Gerhard Maier. I am indebted to Professor Maier for the use of some of his ideas and hope many people will read the work itself. I am indebted to all of the other publications and writers to whom reference has been made in the text for the help they have been to me. And most of all I am indebted to the Billy Graham Evangelistic Association, Billy Graham himself, Cliff Barrows, and George Wilson who have helped to make this book possible.

The Author

Questions Everybody Asks

Introduction—Life's Great Questions

Believe it or not, everybody thinks. Some people may think hardly at all; others may spend much of their lives doing little else. Thinking is related to the asking of questions. And one of the first questions a child asks his mother is this, "Mommy, where did I come from?" That's a good question and we will consider it shortly. But before we do, we need to deal with another important matter. It is this: What *are* life's basic questions?

First of all, we can rule out questions that turn out to be quite unimportant. Among them are the following: "How much money do I have?" "How many houses, lands, and automobiles do I possess?" "Do I have a great reputation?" "How much have I accomplished in life?" "Do people like me?" These are interesting questions that tell us a good deal about how a person has succeeded in life, humanly speaking. But they do not deal with life's most important questions. After all, what difference does it make how much I possess, how great a reputation I have earned, how many friends I have made, and whether I am listed in *Who's Who,* when I'm dead? Death is the great leveler, for we can't take anything with us. We go out the way we came in--empty-handed.

The story is told of Tamerlane, the great conqueror. When he was dying, he gave orders about his burial. He insisted that his hands be raised in the coffin with nothing in them. He wanted all to know that he left as empty-handed as he entered this life. And that is true for all of us. What, then, are life's most important questions?

The first question is, "Who am I?" Today, multiplied numbers of people pay fabulous sums to psychologists and psychiatrists in a vain effort to find out who they are. It is the identity question, the question of personhood. Everyone, sooner or later, one way or another, asks this question.

The second question is, "Where did I come from?" This is the children's question. It has to do with origins. Even children know that there was a time when they were not. And you and I know it too. *Where* did I come from? Am I related to the birds, the flowers, the trees, and the animal order of life? Did I have a pre-existence in some other form? What makes me different from every other form of life and from every other person as well? That's an important question.

The third great question is, "What is the purpose of life?" Stated another way we ask, "Does life have meaning?" "Or is it all a charade?" If life has no purpose, then existence is meaningless. If it does have purpose, what is the purpose?

The fourth of life's basic questions has to do with destiny. "Where do I go when I die?" This introduces many other questions such as "Is there a life after death?" "Where do we go when we die, if there is a life after death?" "What kind of life is there beyond this vale of tears?"

Answers

Strange as it may seem, everybody has answers to these questions. Indeed, there are many different answers and they do not agree with each other at all. When we look at the different answers, it quickly becomes apparent that all of them cannot be true. But the answers diverge so much one from another that any thinking being soon realizes that to believe one is to disbelieve another. It will help us to arrive at answers if we acknowledge one fact. Everybody has presuppositions, known or unknown, when they think about answers to life's basic question. Let's look at a few of the major ones.

The Agnostic Answer

Some people answer these questions by saying, "I don't know." There is a world of difference between saying "I don't know" if you mean by that you can *never* know. To make a statement of this sort is to embrace a presupposition that ultimate reality cannot be apprehended; you can't know it and you can't find it. If that be true, then it is useless to search for that which you can never find. Anyone who makes this statement has become a metaphysician (one who deals with that which is beyond the physical and the experiential). Such a person cannot be an empiricist. For an empiricist deals with what can be seen, felt, handled, and is apparent to the senses. The most a scientist, for scientists are empiricists, can say is that he hasn't found the answers and from his investigations he is doubtful that answers will be forthcoming. But what a true empiricist or scientist cannot say is this, "There is no answer." The moment he does that he has ceased to be empirical and has become a metaphysician and they are quite different kinds of approaches.

It should be said at this point that the great ethnic religions fall into the agnostic category in the sense that they claim that ultimate truth is ineffable. This means ultimate truth cannot be expressed in words; it is indescribable. It is difficult to suppose that a human being can know that which cannot be stated in propositional form. Yet ethnic faiths like Buddhism, Hinduism, and other religions do precisely this.

In 1973 Jacob Bronowski, now dead, published a book, titled *The Ascent of Man* (Boston: Little, Brown and Company), in which he advocated an evolutionary, empirical viewpoint. He opposes authoritarianism of any kind. For him, the empirical approach is the supreme base for his knowledge. But even he must ask the question about man and the future. "What is ahead for us?" he inquires. He replies, "At last the bringing together of all that we have learned, in physics and biology, toward an understanding of where we have come, *what man is* (my italics)....We are *nature's* (whatever that means, for it is nowhere adequately defined) unique experiment to make a rational intelligence prove itself sounder than the reflex. Knowledge is our destiny. Self-knowledge, at last bringing together the experience of the arts and explanations of science, waits ahead of us."

But empiricist Bronowski does have questions he cannot answer. Thus he admits that "the horse and the rider (as an evolutionist) have many anatomical features in common. But it is the human creature that rides the horse, and not the other way around." As one reviewer of his book said: Bronowski "has now experienced death (and this is empirical), and that blind spot is gone. Alas, such an empirical finding cannot be incorporated into a new edition of *The Ascent of Man*." Yes, he now knows the answers to life's most important questions, but for him it is too late!

The Communist Answer

Communism has a clearly defined and carefully articulated world and life view. Make no mistake about that! Communists often put

Christians to shame because they know what they believe, why they believe it, and they can defend it against other options vigorously and often successfully—not because their claims are superior but because they have been trained to present their claims in such a way that they give the appearance of plausibility. And the commitment of individual Communists to the faith they believe in often gives their spurious claims a semblance of attractiveness, because they are ready to die for what they believe.

The Communist has for his basic principle what we call materialism. By this he means that the ultimate reality is matter, not spirit, as the Christian faith proclaims. Because matter is the ultimate reality, the Communist is an atheist. If matter precedes spirit, then spirit must follow matter. And when it does, then whatever follows is the invention of man. In other words, man makes his own gods, but this is an illusion—for there are no gods. And thinking there are gods doesn't make them exist. Thus the primacy of matter rules out the possibility of a God.

The Communist has a second presupposition, that of the dialectic. By this he means that opposites can be reconciled. He does this by presupposing a thesis or existing state which is met head-on by an antithesis, that is, its opposite. In the ensuing struggle between the thesis and the antithesis, out of that struggle there comes into being a synthesis which is the reconciliation of the two opposites. The synthesis then becomes a new thesis, which is challenged by another antithesis, out of which comes a new synthesis. This continues until the paradisaic state is reached and true Communism prevails.

The Communist is saying that man comes from matter, that there is no creator, there is no life after death, and everything belongs to the here and now. He has a narrow creed to be sure, but Communism is a religion and does proclaim it has answers to life's basic questions. For those who are satisfied with those answers, this system can become a way of life. But who thinks in the depths of his heart that these answers are true? And who does not seek for some better answer than that offered by Communism?

The Naturalist or Secularist Answer

The naturalist or secularist answer to life's most important questions can be found in the *Humanist Manifesto II*. It followed hard on the first *Humanist Manifesto* which appeared in 1933, and was superseded by the second one in 1973. This document is plain enough in the claims it makes, and in supplying the presuppositions which undergird this viewpoint. They are non-theists who begin "with humans not God, nature not deity." "Promises of immortal salvation or fear of eternal damnation are both illusory and harmful." "...the human species is an emergence from natural evolutionary forces." "There is no credible evidence that life survives the death of the body." Ethics is "autonomous and situational, needing no theological or ideological sanction." Men have the right to abort babies, get divorces, engage in homosexual activity, and practice euthanasia with the right to suicide. In short, man is an animal, he is part of nature, there is no real purpose for him in life, and there is no life after death. This is the naturalist or secular answer to life's important questions.

The Atheistic Existentialist Answer

At least, the humanist suggests that life may not be totally senseless. The atheistic existentialists, however, carry the humanistic answer to its very logical conclusion. For them, life makes no sense and has no meaning. There is neither creator nor sustainer. Man is caught up in a wilderness from which there is no escape, and there is no hope. He simply must reach out in the midst of this cosmic joke and do the best he can, even though there is no best that he can do. One need only read the writings of Sartre, Camus, Kafka and other existentialists to understand the utter despair that grips them. If indeed life has no meaning, then whatever anyone does makes no difference.

Francis Schaeffer points up one amusing incident in this otherwise black as midnight tale of horror. He mentioned Johnny Cage, the existentialist "chance music" composer who drew notes out of a hat and strung them together. The resultant noise he called music. Believing that life is like that, he quickly discovered that the use of chance operations in another area of life would provide his undoing. He likes mushrooms. But he knows that there are poisonous mushrooms as well as those that are edible. But if he were to use his chance philosophy, he knew he would die by chancing to eat mushrooms that were poisonous. So in hunting for mushrooms he left off the use of chance or random selection of mushrooms lest he die. But if his existentialist views are correct, then death indeed is preferable to life since neither death nor life makes any difference anyhow.

The Relativist Answer

Large numbers of people today are relativists. That is, they do not believe that there are absolutes or things that remain forever the same and forever true. In this view, what one thinks to be true today may be untrue tomorrow. This concept is found deeply imbedded in the western mind and seems to become more prevalent all the time.

One of the best ways to illustrate this world and life view is to paint the legal backdrop against which the issue relates to society and its mores. Oliver Wendell Holmes, a former chief justice of the Supreme Court of the United States, was a leader helping to reshape the judicial system based on relativism. America has now reached the place where, by judicial decision, an action that is legal in one city may be illegal in another. What is right or wrong is determined by what the consensus of any community is concerning the matter. Thus books that are pornographic one place may be nonpornographic in another; homosexual acts in the one community may be banned in one community but accepted in another. In other words, ethics is not based upon any absolute standard that exists outside of man but upon whatever men decide is right or wrong. So whatever is right today may be wrong tomorrow, and vice versa.

When the philosophy of relativism is taken over into the realm of theism, it is easy to see where it can lead. A belief in God today can lead to a disbelief in God tomorrow. The notion of a God who dies for the sins of men can be replaced by its opposite. Man can be a sinner today and a saint tomorrow. He can do the same things he did yesterday. The only change has been in the definition of what a sinner is. When this happens, then right and wrong lose their meaning. Life becomes what you choose to make it. But it leaves behind a series of questions that press for an answer that the relativist cannot supply. The first is philosophic: if the relativist's first principle is true, then he starts with an absolute—i.e., nothing is forever true, except the idea or absolute that "nothing is forever true" is true. This becomes his absolute and the relativist has become an absolutist with a basic inconsistency.

Relativism is the father of anarchy. For if you decide what is right, and I decide that what you claim to be right is wrong, who determines which one of us is right? And why should your right be more acceptable than my wrong? And if the laws of the community are based on the opinions of men, how can there be any acceptable system without forcing someone's convictions on someone else, since nobody's convictions are forever definitive? Even a document like the Constitution of the United States becomes a nightmare. It no longer means what its framers said it means; it only means what each new generation of judges proclaim it to be under changing circumstances. Clearly, relativism is no answer to life's most important questions if for no other reason than that any answer can never be thought to be forever true. And whoever bases his hope of eternal life on that which tomorrow may be false is left without any foundation on which to rest his hope.

Resolving the Dilemma—The Christian Answer

We have posed the problem about life's most important questions and have stated that everybody has some kind of answer to these questions. We have also sketched a few of the many answers to these questions, all of which suffer from serious deficiencies and none of which is really a viable option for a thinking person. For us, the most pressing need is to find answers to the questions. From whence do we get answers that are adequate and that satisfy the inquiring heart?

We turn now to the Christian alternative. But once we do this, we face what at first glance seems an almost impossible quest. We find that even among Christians there are different answers to some of these questions. Which Christian's opinions shall we accept and follow? Some time before his death, Nels Ferré wrote an article in which he stated that Paul Tillich was not a Christian. He went further and said that anyone who was a Tillichian could not be a Christian either. Am I to accept what Nels Ferré said, or what Paul Tillich wrote and said?

We have great names in the roster of the Christian church. But whoever you can name would differ in some of his views from others. We have Augustine, Luther, and Calvin. We have Arminius, Wesley, Edwards, Whitefield, and Moody. To which one of these shall we go to find the answers to life's great questions? Let's put the question another way. What we are really asking is this: What is the source of our religious knowledge? From whence do we get our answers?

This brings us head-on to the major thrust of this work. It involves two questions that cannot be avoided. The first one has just been posed: What is the source for our religious knowledge? But it is followed by a second question that is equally important: Is the source from which we get our knowledge trustworthy? This means that we must go to the right source for our answers, and the source to which we go must be reliable.

It is next to impossible to examine carefully all of the religious writings that exist in the world. Buddhists, Shintoists, Muslims, Taoists, Confucianists, Zoroastrians, Jains, Hindus, and others have their sacred writings. To which of these shall we go for answers? Or to none of them, and why? We do know that Christianity is a religion that differs uniquely from all other religions. We know that its teachings do not agree in principle with any other religions known among men. If it can be demonstrated that Christianity is the true religion, then we need not be concerned with the options that cannot truly be compared with it. Once we have struck gold, we see that all of the other metals are fool's gold that can deceive people into thinking they are the real thing but which, upon close examination, prove to be false indeed.

So we close this opening chapter by stating plainly that we believe the Bible is the true source of our religious knowledge. And we do not hesitate to make the claim that the Bible is a reliable book. To these subjects we now address ourselves.

The Bible - the Source of Our Religious Knowledge

The Bible is the starting point, or the source, of our religious knowledge. Once we have said this, we must then ask what the Bible's presuppositions are. After we have analyzed the presuppositions we can determine what the Bible teaches us about the important questions of life.

The Self Revelation of God — God Is

The first presupposition of the Bible is its claim that God is. The Bible itself does not spend precious time trying to prove the existence of God. It simply starts with this great affirmation: God is! We all have heard of the various philosophic arguments used by scholars to develop an apologetic for the fact that God is, as the Bible claims. They include the ontological, the teleological, and the cosmological arguments for the existence of the divine being. We do not need to consider them here, even though they do supply us with helpful ammunition when we approach agnostics or even atheists. But we must never forget that all of the arguments for the existence of God will not avail unless the person to whom they have been given approaches God by faith. The Bible teaches us distinctly that salvation is not attained by knowledge, although some knowledge is essential. We are saved by faith, the third aspect of which is a reaching out to touch the hem of Jesus Christ's garment by an act of will. This involves a decision based on the knowledge of who He is, what He has done, and how He saves us, followed by consent of the mind and appropriated by a decision.

The Bible states categorically that "the fool hath said in his heart, There is no God" (Psalm 53:1). Why does the Scripture say that such a person is a fool? The answer is not hard to find. In order for anyone to make such a statement he must be omniscient, i.e., he must know everything there is to know. If he does not know everything, then the possibility exists that outside the boundaries of his knowledge God might conceivably exist. On the other hand, man who has infinite knowledge and who can affirm there is no God must himself be God. Thus the Bible says that only a fool can assert there is no God.

Affirming that God is, is one thing; to know God as redeemer and savior from sin is another. According to a Gallup Poll made in 1976, ninety-four percent of the people in the United States say they believe in God or a "universal spirit." This can be compared with Canada's 89%, Italy's 88%, Western Europe's 78%, and Japan's 38%. We may conclude that the problem of demonstrating to people that there is a God is not so difficult. Most of them start with the notion that there is one. But acknowledging the existence of a supreme being is hardly enough.

The Bible says that "thou doest well" if you believe that there is one God. But then it adds this significant fact: "The devils also believe, and tremble" (James 2:19). This is an odd statement if it is removed from the biblical context. All James is saying is that belief in the existence of God is step number one toward saving faith. He asserts that the devils who are not saved, and will not be saved, and who will never acknowledge Jesus Christ as Savior, know there is one God. They agree with this notion. But agreement with the notion is insufficient to save them. Men must also reach out in faith and lay hold of Christ.

How God Has Spoken

The fact that God is, does not mean that God of necessity must make himself known to men. Nothing in the lives and circumstances of men or in the nature of God Himself requires Him to disclose Himself to men. Nor is there anything that requires God to disclose Himself in a particular way. What He does is His business. God could disclose Himself as the judge of the whole earth, end the world today, and demand of men an accounting for their sins. He could abandon sinful men to their own pursuits and sit in silence as they destroyed themselves. Men would then have no recourse, for there is no one to whom they could appeal such a verdict. We can be sure that unless God had spoken, men would live and die in darkness and be forever separated from God. But there is a happier side to man's sorry plight. God has made Himself known to men.

The glory of the Christian faith springs from the claim and the truth that the Bible itself is the written self-revelation of God who has spoken in such a way that anyone who comes to the Book by faith can understand the grace of God and the full and free salvation He offers in Jesus Christ His only Son. Later we will show that when God spoke, He did not stutter in His speech. The written Word of God has come to us in accents loud and clear, free from the ambiguities and errors that accompany all other writings of all men for all time. Meanwhile, we must ask the question: How has God spoken?

How God Has Spoken Through Creation

God has spoken, first of all, through natural revelation. All things were made by Him and without Him was not anything made that was made (see Col. 1:16). The writer of the book of Hebrews says that is the One through whom the universe was made (Hebrews 1:2). In other words, there was a time when there was no matter. God is Spirit, not matter. But God by the word of His power called matter into being and made the universe. The Psalmist proclaims that the heavens declare the glory of God and the firmament showeth forth His handiwork (Psalm 19:1). Of all this we must say several things.

The cosmos, that is, the universe, is of great size. In the Space Museum in Washington, D.C., Lindbergh's plane in which he crossed the Atlantic is on display. So is the space ship in which the astronauts flew to the moon. An exhibit in a side room is devoted to a description of the universe. Here it is stated that there are one hundred billion galaxies, and each galaxy has in it a cluster of stars. In each cluster there are a hundred billion stars. Altogether it is estimated that there are 10,000 quintillion stars. Just add eighteen zeroes to the 10,000 and you have the number of stars! And God calls each star by its name. Even more staggering is the fact that the light from some of these stars is 60 quintillion light-years away. Light travels at the rate of 186,000 miles a second. And traveling at that rate of speed it takes 60 quintillion light-years for the light from some of these stars to get to where you and I can see it in the heavens at night.

Nobdoy in his right mind believes that wristwatches happen to come together and that there is no watchmaker behind them. Everyone knows that every watch has a watchmaker. So it is not difficult to perceive that the universe had its creator, the God who called it into being and fashioned it according to the divine plan. There is a fact that we must acknowledge and understand about natural revelation, by which we mean that as a watch denotes a watchmaker so does the world we see denote a creator. What is that important fact?

No man can know God through nature, i.e., through creation. It is not that nature does not make it plain to man that there is a creator. It is only that man cannot find God through nature, even though it witnesses to the divine existence. Man is blinded by sin and cannot read the script of nature. And even if he could read the script of nature, it tells him no more than that there is a God behind it. But it still would not mean that man could then know this God who is behind nature. Thus there is more to God's self-disclosure than natural revelation. There is special revelation, and this revelation consists in two parts: God has revealed Himself in the book we call the Bible, and in Jesus Christ who is the Son of God incarnate.

How God Has Spoken Through the Bible, the Word of God Written

The Bible is the Word of God written. It is the inscripturated Word. It is the source of all the knowledge we have about God. This written Word has come down to us in this form so that all men and every generation can read what God has to say. It is the permanent and enduring Word that has come down to us through the ages, and will always be there for men to see and read. Its nature is such that it can never perish. It will last throughout all the ages of eternity. Of this Word of God written, we shall have more to say in a moment. But we must speak of another Word first.

How God Has Spoken Through Jesus Christ, the Word of God Incarnate

God not only has spoken through nature and through the Bible. He has also spoken through Jesus Christ, who is the incarnate Word. By this we mean that God Himself, in the person of Jesus, assumed human form. He actually became flesh and dwelt among us. He made Himself visible to those who lived at that time, and He has been enshrined in the Bible so that all men of all time can know of this Jesus through the Bible. Indeed, it is a mystery why God should make a beachhead on this tiny planet, which is less than the point of a needle when compared to the vastness of the cosmos. But there is something distinctive about the planet earth. It is the only place where human life exists—where there are men and women made in the image of God (we call it the *imago dei*).

The earth is also the scene of a great disaster. The first man, Adam, sinned against God and was driven from the Garden of Eden.

But more than that, he was estranged from his Creator and separated in such a way that he could not be reconciled unless and until the penalty for man's sin was paid. The righteousness of God had to be vindicated, if a way back to God was to be opened up. This is the reason why God sent His only begotten Son. This is the reason for the cross of Calvary. This is the reason why salvation comes from the crimson flow of blood from the wounded Savior's brow and side. It made our salvation possible and brought with it the gift of eternal life for those who believe on Jesus.

The Relation of the Two Words

Right now we must forever remember one truth that is of supreme significance in the Christian faith. The two Words of God are inextricably and forever interrelated. They cannot be separated. If they are separated, then we lose both of them. They stand or fall together. The only incarnate Word we can know, the only incarnate God who has revealed Himself *in* Scripture is the Jesus *of* Scripture. There is no other Jesus than the biblical Jesus. Somehow this truth must be imprinted on our minds and hearts so indelibly that we will never forget it, nor will we ever let anyone talk to us about any other Jesus than the biblical Jesus. Of course, men do write books about Jesus. The Apostle John says that the world would not be able to contain all of the books that could be written about the Son of God (John 21:25). But no matter how many books may be written, they are valuable *only* if they are in accord with the one book of which we speak--the Bible. Anyone can write about Jesus so long as he faithfully presents the Jesus of Scripture. To the extent that anyone does this, to that extent he is faithful to the Word of God written. If anyone writes anything about Jesus that does not correspond to the revelation of Jesus given in the Bible, it must be disregarded and put aside as speculative or untrue.

Let's say it another way. First, the Bible is the Word of God. But there is more to it than that. It is the revelation of God to men— by which all the opinions of men must be tested. It is the source for all dogma, and no one shall be asked to believe anything that cannot be found in, or deduced from, the Word of God written. Even the writings of the great Christian leaders of all ages must be tested against the Bible. This is true whether it be Augustine, John Calvin, Martin Luther, or John Wesley. If Augustine wrote anything that contradicts the Bible, then it must be set aside. If John Calvin or Martin Luther asserted anything that cannot be demonstrated from Scripture, we are not called upon to believe it.

The Bible and Our Religious Knowledge

We have said plainly that the Bible is the source of our religious knowledge. But having said that, we must follow it immediately by asserting that Christianity is Christianity, and can be supported and defended only within the context of the Old and the New Testaments. And the truth claims of Christianity are reliable ONLY TO THE EXTENT THAT THE SOURCE FROM WHICH WE DERIVE THESE TRUTHS IS ITSELF RELIABLE. So we are confronted with two major questions: First, "Is the Bible the Word of God?" Second, "Is the Bible the reliable Word of God?" If the revelation of God in Scripture is not reliable, then Christianity can be no more reliable than the source from which it springs. If the premise from which we start is untrue, then the conclusions we draw must be untrue as well. And if we cannot trust the parts of the Bible we can check, why should we trust the parts of the Bible we cannot check? The Christian faith then, stands or falls on the reliability of the revelation of God. So we now turn our attention to the claims the Bible makes about itself, and later to the reasons why we believe these claims to be true.

We have said the Bible is the source of our religious knowledge. As we come to the Bible, certain words that are applied to the Bible must be understood if we are to know what we are talking about. They need not be made so technical that we cannot easily understand what they mean. Yet, at the same time, it would be untrue to suppose that simple explanations exhaust all that the words mean. We know in part and we understand in part. Therefore, only eternity will reveal aspects of these words that none of us has grasped as yet. The words we will discuss are these: authority, revelation, inspiration (verbal, plenary), and inerrancy or infallibility.

Authority

The word "authority" as used here simply means that the Bible stands above us and is believed by us. We accept whatever it teaches us, and practice whatever it commands us. It is the rule of faith and conduct for the Christian. If the Bible is not authoritative, then we are wasting our time and spinning our wheels. Nothing remains to talk about. We must remember that the authority of the Bible is something every Christian accepts voluntarily. It cannot be forced on anyone. In this sense, it is quite different from the authority of the government of the United States or any other government. Citizens of the United States may not like, and indeed may not agree with, the Constitution that governs the nation, but they are required to obey it and penalties are attached if they don't.

Authority and truth must be considered too. In the secular realm, the authority over us may be founded on untruth as in communist lands. But their citizens are bound by this authority even though it may be based on untruths. But the authority of no nation is universal. Thus the Constitution of the United States does not and cannot bind citizens of other lands. It is possible that the constitution of some other nation may be based on truth, but that does not mean it has authority over American citizens.

In the case of the Bible, it claims to have universal authority over all men everywhere. It recognizes that men have what we call the power of contrary choice. They can accept or they can reject the authority of the Bible. They can live by its precepts, or they can refuse to let these precepts bind them. In the realm of the spirit, the Bible makes its unique claims, but it does not employ force to make men either accept or conform to its teachings. Thus its authority is different and unique from all other authorities. It does present men with its sanctions, however, and these should not be overlooked. The sanctions of the Bible are everlasting life and everlasting death. It says to men everywhere that they have the right to choose whether they will put themselves under the authority of the Bible, and they are warned about the consequences that flow from their choices.

Revelation

The authority of the Bible over life is related to its claim to be the revelation of God to men. By revelation we mean that God has made Himself known and this self-disclosure has been inscripturated uniquely in the Bible. We have already mentioned natural revelation, but have said that no man can find God in nature. God, in order for man to find Him, revealed Himself supernaturally, and has done so directly and indirectly.

The Old Testament records how God Himself made personal appearances to selected persons. He appeared as the angel of the Lord; He manifested Himself to men in fire and clouds and smoke; He appeared in the stormy winds. Personal appearances, or theophanies as they are called, reached a climax in the incarnation, when Jesus Christ appeared in human form and lived among men. This was a direct revelation of God in the highest sense.

God has also revealed Himself in direct communications to men in ages past. He did this by audible voice, through dreams, by visions, and even through the Urim and the Thummim. The Holy Spirit, we are told, is the divine author of the Bible, and He it was who revealed the plan of salvation to men who wrote the Word of God that we now have. Some parts of the Bible, such as the Book of the Revelation, were direct communications from God to the writers of Scripture. But there are other places where the Holy Spirit recalled to the minds of men that which He wanted written in the Bible. We can say, then, that the Bible is the revelation of God.

God also disclosed Himself through miracles. These too are revelations of God. We might mention just a few: Creation, the plagues on Egypt, the crossing of the Red Sea, the raising of the dead by Elijah, the miracles of Jesus, the supernatural acts of the apostles, and surely the resurrection of Jesus Himself from the dead by the power of the Holy Spirit.

Note that all of the things we are talking about have come to us through the Bible. It is the sourcebook from which we get all of this information. It claims to be the revelation of God, and we believe that it is. This written revelation of God claims to be the inspired Word of God, and to this we now come.

Inspiration

Multiplied millions of books have been written through the ages. But of all the books that have been written, only one of them is different from all other books. The difference consists in the fact that the Bible is the only book ever written by divine inspiration. No other book can legitimately make this claim; nor is such a claim supportable for any other book, as we shall see later on. The Bible is the kind of book we know it to be by virtue of its being divine revelation. The Bible itself claims to be the inspired Word of God, and the Bible in its entirety is precisely that. We will give our reasons for this in the next chapter. Right now we need to do one thing first.

A definition of inspiration is in order. By inspiration we mean that holy men of God—under the influence and guidance of the Holy Spirit—wrote what God wanted written. The human authors retained their own styles, yet even in the choice of words (verbal inspiration) they were guided by the Spirit; and in writing the Scriptures they were kept from making historical, geological, or scientific errors of any kind. They were preserved from error irrespective of the sources from which they got their information. We do not care whether they got it firsthand as witnesses to the events themselves, whether they got it secondhand from extant records, whether they got it by direct special revelation, or whether they got it by exhaustive investigation--all we are saying is that through the influence of the Holy Spirit, whatever the source of their material, they were enabled to record truth for us, and nothing but the truth.

C.S. Lewis, in *Mere Christianity,* says something that is helpful. Man needs something he hasn't got, and God puts it in him. By way of illustration, he mentions a child who is being taught to write. He says, "...you hold its hands while it forms the letters: that is, it forms the letters because you are forming them." So with Scripture—as fallible, limited human beings sat down to write. The Holy Spirit held their hands, which enabled them to write what they wanted to write, because they wanted to write (but could not by themselves) what the Holy Spirit wanted written.

Inspiration was not mechanical, i.e., the writers were not secretaries who wrote what was dictated to them. Nor was inspiration merely the thoughts or ideas without extending to the words themselves. Thoughts committed to writing must be done through words. If the words are congruent with the ideas, the words, no less than the ideas, take on great significance. In the Bible, sometimes a single word makes all the difference about what is to be conveyed. So even the words (verbal inspiration) are an integral part of inspiration.

Some people hold that the term inspiration only means genius of a high order. They say that the writers of Scripture were no more inspired than Milton, Mohammed, Shakespeare, Buddha, or other well-known authors. Thus, they do not think the Bible is really unique and alone among the books of men. Still others think that even as men like the Apostle Paul were inspired to write, so Christians in every age have enjoyed similar inspiration. Thus, there would be no reason why another Bible could not be written today.

Sometimes inspiration is confused with illumination. They are distinctly different. Illumination has to do with the understanding of the Bible, not with the writing of it. The Bible gives us objective knowledge, but the eyes of men are blinded so that they cannot understand the Bible without the help of the Holy Spirit. Paul in 1 Corinthians 2 says this, "The man without the Spirit does not accept the things that come from the Spirit of God, for they are foolishness to him, and he cannot understand them, because they are spiritually discerned."

We have said that the Bible claims to be authoritative, that it is God's revelation, that all of it is inspired (plenary), and that inspiration pertains to the very words of Scripture (verbal inspiration) as well as the ideas. So the task that remains is to explain what we mean by inerrancy or infallibility.

Inerrancy or Infallibility

Inerrancy and infallibility are synonymous terms: they mean the same thing. Yet it is true that some people try to assert that there is a difference. We must know clearly what the purported difference is. Those who distinguish between the two terms do so by saying in effect that the Bible is infallible, but it is not inerrant. By this they generally mean that the trustworthiness of the Bible is limited to matters of faith and practice. Or they mean that the Bible infallibly does its work of salvation. On these matters the Bible is trustworthy. But they think that inerrancy, and they are right, claims that ALL of the Bible is trustworthy, even in matters that may not be intrinsic to salvatory matters of faith and conduct. In other words, the Bible cannot be trusted in matters of science, cosmology, and history.

Most of those who hold to limited infallibility refuse to assert that the Bible is the infallible Word of God. They carefully say that "the Bible is the Word of God, the only infallible rule of faith and practice." By stating it this way, they are being careful not to say that *all* of the Bible is infallible or inerrant. To them, inerrancy means infallibility in the whole and in the parts of the Bible; whereas infallibility for them means that trustworthiness is limited to matters of faith and conduct consonant with the saving purpose of God.

In the history of the Christian Church, its testimony through the ages has been in favor of biblical inerrancy. Of this, more will be said later. Moreover, the men God has used most through the centuries in evangelism and missions have believed the Bible to be true in all of its parts.

When we started, we said that there are two important questions that must be asked when we try to get answers to life's basic questions. One is: "What is the source of my religious knowledge?" The second is: "Is the source of my religious knowledge trustworthy?" We have claimed forthrightly that the Bible is the only source of our religious knowledge; and, in dealing with inerrancy or infallibility, we are saying that the Bible is the wholly *trustworthy* source of our religious knowledge. We are also saying that once you dilute this claim to complete trustworthiness you open the floodgate to doubt about all parts of the Bible. And the history of the Church shows that once infallibility or inerrancy is compromised other great doctrines of the Christian faith suffer as well.

There are some things we are not saying. We are not saying that the Bible is inspired because it is inerrant. Nor are we saying that it is revelation because it is inerrant. We are saying that inspiration, if it means anything, means that the Bible must be inerrant. This turns on the question of what inspiration means. If inspiration does not mean the conveyance of truth, then it must mean the conveyance of error, or at least a combination of truth and error. Since every book in the world that has ever been written apart from the Bible has truth and error in it, in what way would the Bible differ from all other books? And would this not empty the term "inspiration" of any solid or real meaning? Moreover, it is true that even those who limit infallibility to some part of Scripture, do admit that that part is inspired truth, even as the other part is inspired error. Thus we find ourselves in the predicament of believing a doctrine of the inspiration of all of Scripture, but limiting inspiration by saying it does not carry truth with it in everything, only truth in matters of faith and conduct. Once this is done, the doctrine of inspiration has been compromised. For if part of the inspired Bible is not true, how then can we know what part is true, and who determines which is which?

Moreover, there is absolutely nothing in the Bible itself--and even those who hold to limited infallibility must say this--which says that parts of the Bible are inspired and parts are not inspired, or that some things are true and others are not true. The Bible itself deals with the Bible as a whole; and even though there may seem to be problems from a human perspective, yet the Bible itself allows for no errors in it.

The Autographs

In a moment, we will be addressing ourselves to the reasons why we believe that the Bible is free from all error in the whole and in the parts. But before we do that, one other item needs attention. This has to do with what we call the original manuscripts of the Bible, or the autographs. We do not have the autographs of the Bible, Old and New Testaments. We only have copies that have come down to us through the ages. Most statements about biblical infallibility say that the Bible is inerrant in the autographs. Immediately the critics exclaim that we cannot prove inerrancy, since we do not have the original writings. And they try to make much of this. They say we are talking about what does not exist. We only have the copies before us. But they do this because they reject inerrancy and, in effect, say that there are errors in the autographs they don't have either! Thus, neither those who claim the Bible has errors in it nor those who claim it doesn't, can establish the case on the basis of autographs neither possesses. So we have to go at it another way.

The question about the autographs must be divided into two parts. The first has to do with the Old Testament Scriptures. There are very few copies of the Old Testament in existence compared to the New Testament. We do know, of course, that the canon of the Old Testament was known in Jesus' day, and that the same books we have in our Old Testament are the books Jesus had. Since fewer manuscripts are available, for copyists usually destroyed the old scrolls once they were copied, there is little to check against. That is one reason why the discovery of the Dead Sea Scrolls was important. It did give us something against which to check the manuscript evidence we do have. The Dead Sea Scrolls confirmed the fact that the Old Testament as we have it is remarkably accurate. If there are problems, they are not problems of different manuscripts saying different things. But we will leave the argument for the trustworthiness of the Old Testament for the next chapter, when we give reasons for believing the Bible to be trustworthy. This brings us to the New Testament.

There are literally thousands of pieces of the New Testament Scriptures available for study. In fact, the Sinaiticus manuscript contains all of the New Testament canon. Lower criticism's function is to establish what the original text of the New Testament really is. This work has progressed far enough so that very little remains by way of textual problems for the New Testament. There are variant readings in the different manuscripts, but scholars have worked their way through the problems and have arrived at a point where a scholar by the name of Dr. Palmer of the New York Bible Society can assert that we have reached 98 percent certainty with regard to the New Testament text.

Westcott and Hort, in their book, *The New Testament in Greek,* say, "If comparative trivialities, such as changes of order, the insertion or omission of the article with proper names, and the like, are set aside, the words in our opinion still subject to doubt can hardly amount to more than a thousandth part of the whole New Testament" (p. 565).

F.F. Bruce, a well-known New Testament scholar, said, "The variant readings about which any doubt remains...affect no material question of historic fact or of Christian faith and practice." One of the reasons why those of us who believe in biblical inerrancy refer to the autographs is this. There are some words and a few verses, and even one or two passages, of the New Testament about which there are questions whether they were in the autographs. Since we do not have absolute proof one way or the other--either that these were or were not in the autographs—and since we are commanded neither to add to nor take away from the Word of God, it would be unwise to make assertions about these few passages. But what is important to remember is this. Those parts about which there is any question have nothing to do with the question of error. Their inclusion or their exclusion would not take away biblical inerrancy, for they would not be telling us anything that was false or untrue.

One further word about the autographs of Scripture is in order. Critics frequently allude to the indisputable fact that we do not have the original autographs. Somehow they feel this destroys the case for an inerrant Bible. What the fail to consider is this: What they say about the Word of God written is also true about the Word of God incarnate. We, today, have not seen the Son of God any more than we have seen the autographs of Scripture. The apostle Peter spoke of the second coming of the Lord Jesus, "Whom having not seen, ye love; in whom, though now ye see him not, yet believing, ye rejoice with joy unspeakable and full of glory" (1 Peter 1:8). We have not seen Jesus yet, but we will someday. If we can believe in Him whom we have not seen, why can't we also believe in the autographs of Scripture we have not seen either?

Before we state the reasons why we believe the Bible to be true in all of its parts, it would be helpful to note what one great theologian had to say about the autographs.

Professor William G.T. Shedd was a colleague of Charles Augustus Briggs at Union Theological Seminary in New York City. Dr. Briggs was a champion of biblical errancy; Dr. Shedd championed inerrancy. Dr. Briggs made light of the idea that the original autographs (which, he pointed out, we do not have) were without error. Dr. Shedd had this to say:

Why did not God inspire the copyists as well as the original authors? Why did He begin with absolute inerrancy, and end with relative inerrancy? For the same reason that, generally, He begins with the supernatural and ends with the natural. For illustration, the first founding of His Church, in both the Old and New dispensations, was marked by miracles; but the development of it is marked only by His operations in nature, providence, and grace. The miracle was needed in order to *begin* the Kingdom of God in this sinful world, but is not needed in order for its continuance and progress.

And the same is true of the revelation of God in His written Word. This must *begin* in a miracle. The truths and facts of revealed religion, as distinguished from natural, must be supernaturally communicated to a few particular persons especially chosen for this purpose. Inspiration comes under the category of the miracle. It is as miraculous as raising the dead. To expect, therefore, that God would continue inspiration to copyists after having given it to prophets and apostles, would be like expecting that because in the first century He empowered men to raise the dead, He would continue to do so in all centuries.

If this had been necessary, if God could not have extended and perpetuated His Church without the continuance of miracles, doubtless He would have wrought miracles perpetually; for we cannot suppose that Omnipotence would suffer itself to be defeated in any undertaking. But whatever can be accomplished by His ordinary methods in nature, providence, and grace, God so accomplishes.

Now, this applies to divine revelation. The Scriptures could not have been originated and written down in the vernacular of the prophets and apostles without an inerrant and infallible inspiration, and as thus originated and written they were perfect, containing no error. God the Holy Spirit inspires no error, great or small. This is a miracle.

But these Scriptures can be copied into thousands of manuscripts, so that these shall substantially reproduce the autographs in doctrine, history, physics, chronology, geography; in short, in everything that goes to make up the Scriptures. This latter process is not supernatural and preclusive of all error, but providential and natural and allowing of some error. But this substantial reproduction, this relative "purity" of the original text as copied, is sufficient for the divine purposes in carrying forward the work of redemption in the world.

But had the employment of this method of special providence involved the radical alteration of the original autographs, so as to introduce essential and fatal error into them, then doubtless it would not have been employed, but the copyists as well as the prophets and apostles would have been supernaturally "moved by the Holy Ghost," and their copies would have been exact *facsimiles* of the autographs.

One or the other view of the Scriptures must be adopted; either that they were originally inerrant and infallible, or that they were originally errant and fallible.

The first view is that of the Church in all ages: the last is that of the rationalist in all ages.

He who adopts the first view, will naturally bend all his efforts to eliminate the errors of copyists and harmonize discrepancies, and therefore bring the existing manuscripts nearer to the original autographs. By this process, the errors and discrepancies gradually diminish, and belief in the infallibility of Scripture is strengthened.

He who adopts the second view, will naturally bend all his efforts to perpetuate the mistakes of scribes, and exaggerate and establish discrepancies. By this process, the errors and discrepancies gradually increase, and disbelief in the infallibility of Scripture is strengthened.

That the theory of the original errancy and fallibility of Scripture as it came from the prophets and apostles should be maintained and defended by the rationalistic critic, is comprehensible--his hostility to the supernatural explains it--but that it should be maintained and defended by professedly evangelical critics, is inexplicable, except on the supposition that they do not perceive the logical result of the theory, and its exceedingly destructive influence upon the belief of mankind in divine revelation (*Calvinism: Pure and Mixed* [Scribner, 1893], pp. 140-142).

Why We Believe the Bible Is True

We believe that the Bible is free from all error in the whole and in the parts for a number of good reasons. In recounting them, it should be remembered that the order in which we list them has nothing to do with the importance of each of them. Moreover, even if we were to eliminate every consideration and make no case for the trustworthiness of the Bible, it still would be true. In and of itself, the Bible stands and is true. In this sense, it is similar to the evidences we might adduce for the existence of God. Whether or not we give reasons why we believe God exists in no way changes the fact that He is. So also with Scripture and its truthfulness. It is self-evident and does not need to be demonstrated. But men, being what they are, do look for supportive reasons to validate what the Bible claims for itself and what men know intuitively to be true.

If we put the issue another way, it may be clearer yet. Once we suppose the existence of God, and once we allow that God has spoken, we know immediately that He cannot and does not speak untruth. Nor is He limited in His self-disclosure, so that when He used human vessels through whom to communicate, the resulting product must be marred by their frailties. The human writers of Scripture were sinners. They were finite and they could err. But He who is divine, infinite, and unerring, could and did work through men to produce a Bible that bears the humanity of men but not the errors of men. Thus the Bible is both divine and human in origin, but its humanity cannot mean that God was forced to limit His activity so as to give us a book that is partly true and partly false.

Theological Liberals deny the trustworthiness of the Bible in theological as well as other matters. Virtually all others agree that the Bible is true, at least in matters having to do with salvation.

This limited inerrancy is fatal for several reasons. One we have already stated: it makes God the author of error; i.e., He accommodates Himself to the finitude of men and their inability to give us a book completely free from error. The question these people have never answered satisfactorily is this: If God could so move the writers of Scripture to give us a salvation message that does not err, why suppose that He did not do the same about what they sometimes call non-revelational matters? If, in order to give us such a book that is errorless, He was forced to use the human authors in such a way that they somehow lost their independence and became mere secretaries, does not answer the question. Certainly, He must have done at least something similar to this to keep them from writing theological falsehoods. And if He overruled their independence at this point, why balk at the idea that He could not, or should not, have done so in supposedly less important matters? Once the principle of divine interference is accepted as part of the inspiration process, human freedom has been abridged to the extent that this is so. The authors had to write what God wanted written. Why then limit the extent of the divine participation to certain parts of Scripture, especially since the Bible itself witnesses to the fact that *all* Scripture is inspired?

Limited inerrancy is fatal for another reason. It exalts the humanity of Scripture above the divine. Any cursory reading of articles and books written about a partially errant Bible quickly discloses the not-too-hidden presupposition employed by people who deny biblical inerrancy. They talk speciously about the intention of the authors of Scripture. And when they do this, they always have the human authors in mind--whether it be Moses, Paul, Peter, John, etc. In so doing, they obscure the important fact that Scripture has its origins in God, not in man. God is the real author of Scripture, as the Baptist New Hampshire Confession says. And were it not for God's initiative there would have been no Scripture. Even the most vocal opponents of inerrancy are still forced to say that it was the Holy Spirit who inspired the writers of the Bible.

To make men and God co-equal in the writing of the Bible may be one of the great blunders of our day. God did use men to accomplish the divine purpose, but that purpose was the purpose of God and not the purpose of men. Any biblical author's only purpose in writing Scripture was to make himself available to the Holy Spirit to get written what the Holy Spirit wanted written. God graciously condescended to use the inbuilt (which He built in them in the first place) abilities of the authors to accomplish the divine purpose. Thus, to speak of the intention of the author and to leave out the intention of God is a grievous fault. We must therefore insist that God used men to get what He wanted done. At the same time, He did so without fatally compromising their humanity, or forcing them to write that which was contrary to their wills.

Surely no one will accuse a pianist, who renders his version of Chopin his way, of being a robot whose integrity has been sacrificed on the altar of dictation, such as some scholars say must be true for anyone who believes in verbal inspiration and the inerrancy of all of the Bible. The musician who plays Chopin does so of his own will, and brings to bear upon Chopin his understanding of the piece Chopin wrote. The writers of the Bible chose to yield themselves to the Holy Spirit of God, and in so doing became His vessels for the divine use. They were faithful exponents of the divine composition and assisted the Holy Spirit in accomplishing what the Holy Spirit set out to do. The Spirit played a primary role, not a secondary one. And any view of Scripture which attributes a role to the human authors co-equal to that of the Holy Spirit loses sight of this great truth. Scripture is "God-breathed" not "man-breathed." It was God's Word that came through man's pen. "Holy men spoke as they were moved by the Holy Spirit." The Holy Spirit did not speak as He was moved by men!

The Evidences

Now we must set forth some of the reasons why we believe that the Bible is inerrant. And we start first with the Holy Spirit and His witness to Scripture.

The Witness of the Holy Spirit

The person and work of the Holy Spirit has received more attention in our day than perhaps in any decade in the twentieth century. This is all to the good, for the Bible indicates that from Pentecost onward we have been in the age, or the dispensation, of the Holy Spirit. *The Acts of the Apostles* might easily be subtitled *The Works of the Holy Spirit,* or *The Acts of the Holy Spirit.* Some who do not believe in biblical inerrancy talk about the witness of the Holy Spirit. But they do it in a subjective fashion. Someone has written, "What proof do we need, to know whether the Bible is the Word of God? Nothing but the Spirit of God speaking to us in Scripture." When this turns out to mean that there are errors in Scripture, it becomes an exercise in futility. Believers in biblical infallibility should not then discard the witness of the Spirit, for it was part and parcel of the Reformation heritage of Protestants.

The *Westminster Confession of Faith* (of which we will say more later), one of the great confessions of all times, has this to say about the Spirit and the Word:

Our full persuasion and assurance of the infallible truth, divine authority thereof (i.e., of the Bible), is from the inward work of the Holy Spirit, bearing witness by and with the Word in our hearts (I:iv).

John Calvin in his *Institutes of the Christian Religion* said this:

The testimony of the Holy Spirit is superior to all reason...It is necessary therefore, that the same Spirit who spake by the mouths of the prophets, should penetrate into our hearts, to convince us that they faithfully delivered the oracles which were divinely entrusted to them...Let it be considered, then, as an undeniable truth that they who have been inwardly taught by the Spirit, feel an entire acquiescence in the Scripture, and that it is self-authenticated, carrying with it its own evidence, and ought not to be made the subject of demonstration and arguments from reason; but it obtains the credit which it deserves with us by the testimony of the Spirit...(and) we submit our judgments and understandings as to a thing concerning which it is impossible for us to judge... because we feel the firmest conviction that we hold an invincible truth.

Now we must examine the implications of this witness of the Holy Spirit, whose witness we acknowledge and accept with fervent gratitude. But this does not mean that we are left without any problems. The chief problem which we face immediately is this: "Can the Holy Spirit witness to some that the Bible is inerrant, and to others that the Bible is errant in some of its parts?" The answer is so obvious that it hardly needs to be stated. Of course, the Holy Spirit cannot witness, speaking anthropomorphically, out of both sides of the divine mouth at the same time. The Holy Spirit is truth, and cannot lie. Therefore, the Holy Spirit cannot witness to opposite propositions. Somebody must be wrong. Who is wrong and how can we tell?

The strange aspect of this problem is that those who deny biblical inerrancy do not openly say they have the witness of the Holy Spirit that the Bible is partly untrue, even if only in matters that do not relate to faith and practice. But if the witness of the Holy Spirit means anything, and if by His witness they accept some parts as true, then it must be by His same witness that they acknowledge those things they think are not true. Let them come out boldly and say that the Spirit has witnessed to them that parts of the Bible are untrue. If they do this, then we will be able to deal with matters at the right point and from the proper perspective. Unless they are willing to say this, they have adopted an untenable position. They are then saying parts of the Bible are untrue because they have evidence outside of the Bible which causes them to make this decision. They pass human judgment on the Word of God. In that event, the Bible is subordinated to human authority, whereas the plain teaching of the Word of God is that it stands above and beyond all principalities and powers—including scholars.

We cannot help but be deeply impressed that current emphases on the witness of the Holy Spirit lend themselves to a subjectivism that is closely akin to the modern existential mood. Subjectivism is dangerous, for its validity resides in the feelings of each individual. It becomes detached from an outside objective framework of reference against which feelings can be tested. The Bible is objectively there and objectively true, whether I feel like it or not. The Bible is still true, even when men do not have the witness of the Spirit or reject that witness. Therefore, we must impress upon our consciousness several facts that help us to guard against experiences that may be invalid. The Westminster Confession of Faith, when it speaks about the witness of the Holy Spirit, provides safeguards against subjectivism by emphasizing objective realities against which experience can be checked. The Confession says that the work of the Holy Spirit is to bear witness to our spirits "by and with the Word in our hearts." There is, therefore, a coordinate witness—that of the Word of God written, and of the Holy Spirit. We should remember that whatever we know about the Holy Spirit in the first place we have learned from Scripture. It is Scripture that tells us who the Holy Spirit is and what work He performs. And one of His works is to bear witness to us that the Bible, from which we get our knowledge of Him and of the plan of salvation, is true.

The Holy Spirit can only bear witness in accord with the Word of God. Therefore, the Holy Spirit cannot bear witness to us that the Bible has errors in it, when the Bible proclaims itself to be free from error.

Two possible objections can be made at this point. Someone can say that the Bible itself teaches there are errors in Scripture. If that can be established then, of course, the issue is foreclosed. But no one has ever yet shown that the Bible so teaches this. The second objection can be raised that perhaps the Bible does not teach one way or the other about its inerrancy. But as we have said previously, even those who dislike full inerrancy do admit that at least the Bible does teach and make a claim for inerrancy about matters of faith and practice. But since the Scripture they use to support this claim plainly includes ALL of Scripture, and does not limit itself to a PART of Scripture, they have lost their case. But even *if* the Scripture did not make a claim for plenary inerrancy, the burden of proof from Scripture—and not from something alien brought to bear on Scripture—would be required to show that a Bible with error can be logically deduced from the phenomena of Scripture. This cannot be done, so that the claim to inerrancy is secure.

Scripture also teaches us that we are to try every spirit. And this all-embracing command cannot exclude trying the Holy Spirit, to be sure that we are not listening to a demon rather than the Spirit of God. How can we test the spirits? Obviously, it must be done by referring to something outside of us. And what is it that we have outside of us to which we can go, and by which we can test the spirits? Plainly, it is to the written Word of God. So we come full circle once more to Scripture, which is the rod or rule by which all the opinions *and* the experiences of men can be tested.

At the Bureau of Standards, the United States Government maintains the official weights and measures standards for the nation under controlled conditions. There the government has yardsticks, pounds, and fractions thereof. All weights and measures are tested against the unvarying standards which have been set up there. And that is why the scales in our supermarkets bear seals to show they have been tested against the standards, to make certain that we are not short-weighted when we buy our fruits and vegetables, or meats. In a way far beyond anything so incidental as this, God has ordained that His Word shall be the official standard against which everything pertaining to the Christian faith, and anything about which God has chosen to speak, may be tested.

The Spirit witnesses to our spirits. This we claim to be true. But He witnesses to our spirits in and through the Word of God. And that which the Spirit witnesses to, says John Calvin, is the Word of God written, to which we submit ourselves in entire acquiescence for "it obtains the credit which it deserves with us by the testimony of the Spirit."

The Witness of Jesus

The second reason why we believe that the Bible is true in all of its parts is that Jesus Christ Himself taught this in the Scriptures. Along with the Holy Spirit, He is a supreme witness for this claim.

Jesus Christ is the author of our salvation. He is the Son of God to whom we come for salvation. He is the Lord of our lives. And Lordship means that we believe Him and all that He said and taught. We accept whatever He said as being true, for He could not lie. Our attitude toward the Bible should be the attitude of the Lord Jesus. If it is anything less than that, we have a defective Christology and we have reduced Jesus Christ to something less than God when we adopt views that are at variance with His teaching.

A quick look at some of the Scriptures in which the words of Jesus concerning biblical inerrancy appear should help us see what the Master thought and taught. In John 10:35, Jesus said "scripture cannot be broken." Clearly, He was talking about the Old Testament and was placing His imprimatur on it. Matthew Henry says in his commentary, "We are sure that the Scripture *cannot be broken*, or broken in upon, or found fault with. Every word of God is *right;* the very style and language of Scripture are unexceptionable, and not to be corrected, Matt. 5:18" (Vol. V, p. 1040, Revell NY N.D.). Jesus was not talking about a limited part of the Old Testament. He was speaking about a specific statement in the Old Testament, but He based His belief in that verse on the fact that the totality of Scripture cannot be broken. And if no part of Scripture can be broken, then the one verse to which He makes reference cannot be broken either. But if a single verse can be nullified there is no reason, in principle, why others cannot also be set aside.

The frequent and unvarying testimony of Jesus in the Gospels certifies the fact that He trusted the Bible in all of its parts. In John 5:39, Jesus is speaking about the witness of the Father to Himself. He turns the attention of His listeners to a fact that they agreed with and with which He was in agreement also. He said, "Ye search the scriptures, because you think that in them you have eternal life." If He Himself did not agree with this proposition, He certainly would have shown them the error of their ways and pointed them in the direction of the true truth outside of the Old Testament. Instead, He adds these words which certify His own convictions about the Old Testament, "It is they that bear witness to me." And later He concludes, "If you believed Moses, you would believe me, for he wrote of me. But if you do not believe his writings, how will you believe my words?" (5:46f.). Here Jesus bases the truth of His own words on the truth of Moses' words!

In the high priestly prayer of Jesus in John 17, He intercedes with the Father for His own disciples. His petition is, "Sanctify them in the truth" (vs. 17). That is, Jesus wants them to have the truth, the whole truth, and nothing but the truth. And He adds these words,

"Thy word is truth." What words can He be speaking of if not the words of the Scriptures, i.e., of the Old Testament? There is no hint of a Scripture that is partly true and partly false. No word of reservation. Rather, there is the identification of the Scripture of the Old Testament as the Word of God. And it is truth.

In a rather casual incident, the words of a bystander are turned in the direction of the Word of God written. A woman in a crowd "raised her voice and said to him, 'Blessed is the womb that bore you, and the breasts that you sucked' " (Luke 11:28). Jesus immediately used these words to make an important point. He said, "Blessed rather are those who hear the word of God and keep it" (vs. 28). There would be no point in urging people to hear the Word of God, if the Word they heard was not true. It would be less compelling for them to keep the Word of God unless it was true. Another instance coincides with this one. Subsequent to His resurrection, Jesus is instructing His disciples. Luke records this fact, "Then he opened their minds to understand the scriptures" (Luke 24:45). And He did so not to depreciate them but to show how they were accurate and truthful witnesses to Him and to His mission.

In the Sermon on the Mount, Jesus spoke some of His strongest words about the eternity of the Old Testament and His own relationship to the Word of God written. He said, "Think not that I have come to abolish the law and the prophets; I have not come to abolish them but to fulfill them" (Matthew 5:17). In this statement, Jesus was talking about the totality of the Old Testament which comprised the law and the prophets. The King James version reads, "Think not that I am come to destroy the law, or the prophets; I am not come to destroy, but to fulfill." The verb "destroy" or "abolish" means to "loosen down" as of a house or tent (see 2 Cor. 5:1). "Fulfill," says A.T. Robertson, "is to fill full. This Jesus did to the ceremonial law which pointed to Him and the moral law He kept." Not only is Jesus not about to destroy or abolish the law and the prophets, He is not even going to loosen them. So great is the point He made that Jesus goes on to assert, "For truly (the word truly is "amen" in the Greek), I say to you, till heaven and earth pass away, not an iota, not a dot, will pass from the law until all is accomplished" (Matt. 5:18). A.T. Robertson in his *Word Pictures in the New Testament* says this:

> One jot or one tittle (*iota hen e mia kerea*). "Not an iota, not a comma" (Moffatt), "not the smallest letter, not a particle" (Weymouth). The iota is the smallest Greek vowel, which Matthew here uses to represent the Hebrew *yod* (jot), the smallest Hebrew letter. "Tittle" is from the Latin *titulus* which came to mean the stroke above an abbreviated word,

then any small mark. It is not certain here whether *kerea* means a little horn, the mere point which distinguishes some Hebrew letters from others or the "hook" letter *Vav*. Sometimes *yod* and *vav* were hardly distinguishable. "In *Vay*. R. 19 the guilt of altering one of them is pronounced so great that if it were done the world would be destroyed" (McNeile). (Broadman: Nashville, 1930, Vol. I, p. 43.)

One is hard put to go beyond what Jesus says here. And what He says should be sufficient to guide us into His viewpoint and understanding of the sanctity, truth, and eternality of the Word of God written.

What we have said about Jesus regarding the Old Testament, we must now say about the New Testament which was not yet written when Jesus spoke on earth. In John 16:13, Jesus pre-authenticated the New Testament. He said, "When the Spirit of truth comes, he will guide you into all the truth; for he will not speak of his own authority, but whatever he hears he will speak, and he will declare to you the things that are to come." Matthew Henry says about this:

> He will take care that they (the disciples) do not miss their way: *He will guide you*; as the camp of Israel was guided through the wilderness by the *pillar of cloud and fire*. The Spirit guided their tongues in speaking, and their pens in writing to secure them from mistakes.
>
> (He shall guide them) into nothing but the truth. All that *he shall guide you into shall be truth* (1 John 2:27); *the anointing is truth.*
>
> Men's word and spirit often disagree, but the eternal Word and eternal Spirit never do. (*Ibid.*, p. 1139)

The words of Jesus pre-authenticating the New Testament Scriptures tell us that there was to be further revelation, and the fact that Jesus said it was the Holy Spirit who would call all things to their remembrance concerning Him is supportive of the biblical claims that indeed the Holy Spirit moved the apostles to write the Books of the New Testament. The Church councils did not decide what was, and was not, inspired by the Holy Spirit. All they did was to acknowledge what was apparent to the churches, and had been accepted by the churches in the early church period. Multitudes of early church writings were never regarded by the congregations as coming from God the Holy Spirit. But that which was received, used, and accepted from the beginning was recognized by the Church councils to be the Word of God written and canonical.

John Warwick Montgomery, a brilliant evangelical scholar, said this with regard to Jesus and Scripture:

Christ's attitude toward the Old Testament was one of *total trust;* nowhere, in no particular, and on no subject did he place Scripture under criticism. Never did he distinguish truth "in faith and practice" from veracity in historical and secular matters, and he told the Evil Foe in no uncertain terms that man lives "by *every word* that proceedeth out of the mouth of God" (Matt. 4:4, quoting Deut. 8:3). To his apostles, under whose scrutiny the New Testament would be written, he promised his Holy Spirit, who "shall bring *all* things to your remembrance, whatsoever I have said unto you" (John 14:26, cf. 2 Peter 3:15,16).

Inerrancy? Yes. Induction? The way out of the fly bottle? Approaching the Scripture always and everywhere as did the Lord Christ.

From the data about the view of Jesus, we can come to some fair conclusions about His beliefs and His teaching. If Jesus taught biblical inerrancy, either He knew inerrancy to be true, or He knew it to be false but catered to the ignorance of His hearers. Or, He was limited and held to something that was not true, but He did not know it. Whichever way anyone goes with regard to his Christology, certain conclusions follow inevitably. For example, if Jesus knew that the Scripture is not inerrant and yet taught that it is, He was guilty of deception. Thus He was a sinner rather than a sinless being. If He was a man of His times and in ignorance thought inerrancy to be true, then He was in no sense omniscient and this leads to a strange Christology. The third alternative is the only one that holds water. Christ taught that Scripture is inerrant because He knew it to be so. This is the only view that fits the New Testament evidences about the person of Jesus.

The Witness of the Prophets

In addition to the witness of the Holy Spirit and Jesus that the Bible is trustworthy, we have the witness of the prophets and the apostles. We come now to that witness of the prophets, and after that the witness of the apostles.

In Hebrews 1, the Scripture says, "In the past God spoke to our forefathers through the prophets." They were God's mouthpieces; they were the instruments through which He did speak to Israel, and to us today. Again we must note that it is God speaking through them; not they speaking through God. It was not a two-way street; revelation went from God to the prophets, and through the prophets to us. They professed to be proclaiming what God said.

More than two thousand times in one form or another the phrase, "Thus saith the Lord" appears in the Old Testament. This can be illustrated frequently from Scripture. For example, in Isaiah 8, the prophet Isaiah says in verse 1, "The Lord said unto me," and he quotes what God said. In verse 5 he records, "The Lord spake also unto me again, saying," and he quotes what God said. In verse 11 he writes, "For the Lord spake thus to me with a strong hand, and instructed me that I should not walk in the way of this people, saying," and he proceeds to give us the very words of God.

In 2 Samuel 23, the chapter starts with these words, "Now these be the last words of David." But then it goes on to tell us where David got his words, "The Spirit of the Lord spake by me, and his word was in my tongue. The God of Israel spake to me, He that ruleth over men must be just, ruling in the fear of God."

In Jeremiah 46 it says, "The word of the Lord which came to Jeremiah the prophet against the Gentiles." In chapter 47, "The word of the Lord that came to Jeremiah the prophet against the Philistines." In chapter 48, "Against Moab thus saith the Lord of hosts, the God of Israel." In chapter 49, "Concerning the Ammonites, thus saith the Lord." This can be shown to be true throughout Jeremiah's prophecy.

A large part of the book of Isaiah professes to be words given to Isaiah by God, which words he spoke to Israel. In chapter 45, for example, in verse 1, "Thus saith the Lord to his anointed, to Cyrus," and God speaks. In verse 11, "Thus saith the Lord, the Holy One of Israel." In verse 14, "Thus saith the Lord." In verse 18, "For thus saith the Lord." In chapter 49 God says, "I" will do this and that, over and over again. The same use of "I" for God who speaks appears throughout chapter 65. And so it goes, on and on.

The same thing can be said about the prophecy of Ezekiel, "The Lord said to me," "Thus saith the Lord," "He brought me forth," "He brought me to the gate," "The word of the Lord came to me saying." Chapters twelve through eighteen all commence with something like this, "The word of the Lord came to me, saying." The prophecy of Hosea is also punctuated with words directly attributed to Jehovah in conversation with a gainsaying people, "Hear ye this, O priests," "When I would have healed Israel," "Rejoice not, O Israel, for joy, as other people," "Ephraim feedeth on wind," and in the concluding chapter God says, "I will heal their backsliding, I will love them freely."

Nowhere in the Old Testament is there any hint that what is written therein is other than the pure Word of God. Surely it can be summed up in the word from the psalmist who cries out, "For ever,

O Lord, thy word is settled in heaven'' (Psalm 119:89). Change and decay are all around us to be sure. But there are some things that do not change. One of them is the Word of God. What the prophets said, the apostles also said. Their testimony enlarges and expands on the witness of the prophets.

The Witness of the Apostles

The witness of the apostles to the truth of Scripture is perhaps even stronger than that of the prophets of the Old Testament. This statement needs a bit of clarification. We believe in progressive revelation. By this we mean that God did not unfold everything He wanted men to have in the book of Genesis, or in all of the Old Testament. For example, the doctrine of the Church is not found in any fullness in the Old Testament. When we come to the New Testament, we learn many things unknown to the writers of the Old Testament. Moreover, the New Testament book, Hebrews, speaks of some things that—Jesus having come—we no longer need to do. The Levitical sacrificial system involving the shedding of animal blood has been fulfilled in Jesus Christ; they are now abolished. There is, therefore, no more need to offer animal blood for the forgiveness of sins. That which had to be repeated year after year has been done once for all in Jesus Christ. Likewise, we have been given more knowledge concerning the Word of God written in the New Testament where the doctrines of inspiration, revelation, and infallibility or inerrancy are spelled out in greater detail. What is the witness of the New Testament to biblical truthfulness?

In Romans 15:4 the apostle Paul says, ''For whatever was written in former days was written for our instruction, that by steadfastness and by the encouragement of the scriptures we might have hope.'' Paul is here teaching something about all of the former writings. He says they were all written for our instruction. He excludes nothing from the statement and includes everything. He makes no distinction between false and true Scriptures. All of the writings are herein thought to be true. Moreover, Paul uses the same word for Scripture (graphe) which he uses in connection with the next statement of his that we must tackle.

Second Timothy 3:16 is undoubtedly one of the clearest, most explicit statements about biblical trustworthiness to be found in all of the Bible from the theological perspective. Here Paul says, ''All scripture is inspired by God and profitable for teaching, for reproof, for correction, and for training in righteousness, that the man of God may be complete, equipped for every good work.'' While we will be referring to John Calvin later on and quoting from his works when he speaks of Scripture, it will help for us to consider what he says about 2 Timothy 3:16 at this point:

All Scripture; or, *the whole of Scripture*; though it makes little difference as to the meaning. He follows out that commendation which he had glanced at briefly. First, he commends the Scripture on account of its authority; and secondly, on account of the utility which springs from it. In order to uphold the authority of the Scripture, he declares that it is divinely inspired; for, if it be so, it is beyond all controversy that men ought to receive it with reverence. This is a principle which distinguishes our religion from all others, that we know that God hath spoken to us, and are fully convinced that the prophets did not speak at their own suggestion but that, being organs of the Holy Spirit, they only uttered what they had been commissioned from heaven to declare. Whoever then wishes to profit in the Scriptures, let him, first of all, lay down this as a settled point, that the Law and the Prophets are not a doctrine delivered according to the will and pleasure of men, but dictated by the Holy Spirit. If it be objected, "How can this be known?" I answer, both to disciples and to teachers, God is made known to be the author of it by the revelation of the same Spirit. Moses and the prophets did not utter at random what we have received from their hand, but, speaking at the suggestion of God, they boldly and fearlessly testified, what was actually true, that it was the mouth of the Lord that spake. The same Spirit, therefore, who made Moses and the prophets certain of their calling, now also testifies to our hearts, that he has employed them as his servants to instruct us. Accordingly, we need not wonder if there are many who doubt as to the Author of the Scripture; for, although the majesty of God is displayed in it, yet none but those who have been enlightened by the Holy Spirit have eyes to perceive what ought, indeed, to have been visible to all, and yet is visible to the elect alone. This is the first clause, that we owe to the Scripture the same reverence which we owe to God: because it has proceeded from him alone, and has nothing belonging to man mixed with it.

It would be a difficult feat to show that Paul's teaching about the infallibility of Scripture in this passage allows for an interpretation broad enough to include errors in matters other than faith and practice. It would be far more ethical for those who do not believe in biblical inerrancy merely to state that they disagree with Paul than to say that Paul did not teach inerrancy.

Matthew Henry, the great Bible commentator, died before he finished the New Testament. From Romans onward, other writers filled the gap. Benjamin Andrews Atkinson wrote First and Second Timothy. It is obvious that some of what he said came from the Westminster Confession of Faith. He uses the word "Scripture," not "Scriptures," and employs the pronoun "it" when referring to Scripture, not the pronoun "they." This is important because he speaks of the Scripture, that is the Bible in all of its parts, as being infallibly true. Here is an excerpt from what he says:

> The scriptures we are to know are the holy scriptures; they come from the holy God, were delivered by holy men, contain holy precepts, treat of holy things, and were designed to make us holy and to lead us in the way of holiness to happiness; being called the *holy scriptures*, they are by this distinguished from profane writings of all sorts, and from those that only treat of morality, and common justice and honesty, but do not meddle with holiness. If we would know the holy scriptures, we must read and search them daily, as the noble Bereans did, Acts 17:11. They must not lie by us neglected, and seldom or never looked into. Now here observe, (1) What is the excellency of the scripture. It is given by inspiration of God (2 Timothy 3:16), and therefore is his word. It is a divine revelation, which we may depend upon as infallibly true. The same Spirit that breathed reason into us breathes revelation among us: *For the Prophecy came not in old time by the will of man, but holy men spoke as they were moved or carried forth by the Holy Ghost,* 2 Peter 1:21. The prophets and apostles did not speak from themselves, but what they received of the Lord that they delivered unto us. That the scripture was given by inspiration of God appears from the majesty of its style,--from the truth, purity, and sublimity, of the doctrines contained in it,--from the harmony of its several parts,--from its power and efficacy on the minds of multitudes that converse with it,--from the accomplishment of many prophecies relating to things beyond all human foresight,--and from the uncontrollable miracles that were wrought in proof of its divine original: *God also bearing them witness, both with signs and wonders, and with divers miracles and gifts of the Holy Ghost, according to his own will,* Hebrews 2:4.

If the apostle Paul was not writing Scripture, then he surely was guilty of a most high-handed procedure when he made one particular statement to the believers in Thessalonica. He identified the word he spoke as the Word of God. He said, "And we also thank God constantly for this, that when you received the word of God which you heard from us, you accepted it not as the word of men but as what it really is, the word of God, which is at work in you believers"

(1 Thessalonians 2:13). Paul says there are the words of men, and there is the Word of God. His words indeed are the Word of God because they are more than his words. They have their origin in God himsef, who is the author of the divine Word through the human instrumentality.

In 1 Corinthians, Paul claimed to be speaking the wisdom of God. He says that what he spoke had been revealed by the Holy Spirit. And those things had been freely given to him by God, the Holy Spirit being the divine teacher (1 Corinthians 2:11-13). But we must also recall the negative aspect of the Pauline witness. It is the total absence of anything that can be construed as denying the truthfulness of the Word of God that should impress us. Would he not have told us what qualifications he placed on Scripture, if he had any? He did not, because he placed no qualifications and believed the Bible in all of its parts to be true.

The apostle Peter tells us something special about how the Bible was written. He observes that "holy men of God spake as they were moved by the Holy Spirit." The writers were men of God. They did this as they were moved by the Spirit. They did *not* speak if they were not so moved. In other words, no part of Scripture came from the lips or the pens of men in or of themselves. It came only when they were moved by the Spirit. This separates the Word of God written from all other words penned by men which do not participate or share in this divine process.

No one can read any part of the New Testament without being impressed by the fact that the writers convey the sense of divine authority, manifest the badge of truthfulness, and give no impression whatever that what they wrote, or what the other apostles wrote, should or could be doubted by the reader. And no writer gives the impression that what he writes is not to be taken as though it came from the very lips of God Himself.

Does the case of biblical truthfulness stop with the witness of the Holy Spirit, Jesus, the prophets, and the apostles? By no means. There are other evidences that strengthen the viewpoint. Fulfilled prophecy is next in the order of demonstration.

The Witness of Fulfilled Prophecy

Prophecy is one of the major strands of biblical revelation. By prophecy, we usually mean one of two things: the first has to do with the exposition of what the Bible teaches; the other has to do with foretelling what will happen in the future. The latter is the kind of prophecy we have in mind here. The Bible is full of predictive prophecy in which events are spoken of decades or centuries before they actually happened. Obviously, predictive prophecy implies the supernatural and defies human explanation. But such prophecy does demonstrate the divine nature of Scripture. It is difficult to limit oneself to illustrations having to do with predictive prophecy, because there are so many available. Now we need to concentrate on one strand of this formidable web, to demonstrate the point we are making with some of the prophecies concerning Jesus Christ.

Genesis 3:15 refers to the cosmic struggle between God and Satan. The serpent is said to bruise the heel of the redeemer and the redeemer will break the serpent's head. This is a direct reference to Jesus the Messiah. Of this Messiah, the Scripture says that He will come from Abraham's loins. More specifically, He will come from the tribe of Judah--and none other. Of this tribe, He will come from David's loins. Anyone who did not fulfill these requirements could not be the Messiah.

Jesus was to be born in Bethlehem, according to Micah 5:2. He had to come in the fullness of time according to the prophecy of Daniel 11. This was the reason why Herod slaughtered all of the male children in Bethlehem under two years of age. No one born today could be the Messiah. No one born a thousand years ago could have been the Messiah. Only one born within the time scheme of Daniel 11 could be God's anointed. This Messiah was to be called a Nazarene (Matthew 2:23) and "out of Egypt have I called my son" (Matt. 2:13-15 and Hosea 11:1).

The Messiah was to live a sinless life, speak matchless words, die for the sins of mankind, and rise again from the dead. He was to cry out on the cross of Calvary, "My God, my God, why hast thou forsaken me?", "I thirst," and voluntarily give up His own life, for no man could take it from him. He was to be buried in a borrowed tomb, leave behind an outer garment that soldiers would fight over, be despised and rejected of men, and a man of sorrows.

This Man of whom the Scriptures said should be born of the Virgin Mary, suffer under Pontius Pilate, and die an ignominious death, was the only man in history who fulfilled all of the things prophesied centuries in advance of His coming. But there was one prophecy He did not fulfill. The reason for that is simple. It is still future. The Messiah is to come again in power and great glory, at the end of the present age. If He fulfilled all the other prophecies written concerning Him, we can be sure He will fulfill that last prophecy. He will come again!

In addition to fulfilled prophecy, two other witnesses to the truth of Scripture can be adduced. One is archaeology and the other the pragmatic test.

The Witness of Archaeology

Modern biblical critics have always been sceptical of the historical accounts given in the early books of the Old Testament. As a consequence, numerous scholars have said the Old Testament is a "patchwork of popular folk tales and legends." They have said that the statements in the Old Testament cannot be considered as historical, or verifiable. It is here that archaeology has made a dramatic contribution, by way of confirming the amazing accuracy of the Word of God.

We must be careful not to overstretch outselves and pretend that archaeology has done more than it actually has. Hundreds of archaeological sites have never been uncovered, and what has been accomplished by the spade of the archaeologist is only a small segment of what yet remains to be done. But there is sufficient evidence which has come from the work of the archaeologists to reinforce the Christian conviction that the Bible is an historical book, whose statements can be trusted.

Some years ago, the critics looked on the Old Testament accounts of the patriarchs--Abraham, Isaac, and Jacob--with considerable scepticism. Professor S.R. Driver thought they were personifications of tribes. Others regarded them as "reflections of astral deities." Some thought of them as "figures of folk poetry." Today, excavations from such places as Mari and Nuzi have shown that the biblical records are sound.

In Joshua 11, the Scripture says that Joshua took Hazor and destroyed it by fire. Unambiguous evidence has been found. Excavations at Tigael Yadin at Hazor have proved conclusively how accurate the account is in the Book of Joshua. The population of the city was around 40,000. It had defense ramparts close to a hundred feet above a dry moat. It appeared to be impregnable, but Joshua took it and burned it. Edwin Yamauchi in his book, *The Stones and the Scriptures,* speaks of the four feet of "black and ash-filled earth, fallen brick now burned red, and charred and splintered debris." He quotes James Kelso, a well-known archaeologist who commented:

We have never seen indications of a more destructive conflagration in any other Palestinian excavation, a fact which suggests extensive use of wood in Iron I contruction at Bethel. The cultural break between LB (Late Bronze) and Iron I was also more complete than in any other similar break at Bethel...We are compelled to identify it with the Israelite conquest (p. 56).

The kind of evidence mentioned has been repeated again and again in other digs in and around Palestine. It has served to increase the Christian's confidence in the Word of God written. There is no need to go into great detail here, for many available books on the subject cover the matter extensively and with compelling force. But at least one incidental reference to the New Testament is in order, for the same thing has happened for it.

Luke, the author of the third Gospel and the Acts of the Apostles, was an historian. Yet unbelieving commentators have assaulted his accuracy. It occasioned the remark by Deissmann when he was speaking about Luke's use of the Greek word *kyrios*. Critics questioned the correctness of Luke. But it was discovered that the word indeed had been applied to Nero (Acts 25:26). Deissman wrote, "The insignificant detail, questioned by various commentators, who seated at their writing tables of Tübingen or Berlin, vainly imagined that they knew the period better than St. Luke, now appears thoroughly credible." Professor Yamauchi remarks further about Luke's "scrupulous accuracy in describing Paul's appearances before various Roman magistrates," which prompted Sherwin-White to write, "The accounts of these trials in Acts are so technically correct that Roman historians since Mommsen have often used them as the best illustration of Roman provincial jurisdiction in this particular period" (Yamauchi, *op. cit.*, pp. 120,121).

Archaeology is no enemy of the Word of God. It has helped us verify numerous parts of the Old and New Testaments, and has thrown light on dark spots that formerly defied explanation. Its witness to biblical truthfulness and accuracy in matters of detail—as well as in the larger canvas—provides outward, sensible, confirmatory data that support our conviction that the Bible in all of its parts can be trusted.

The Pragmatic Test

One of the evidences for the validity of the Christian faith is the fact that it does what it claims to do. Any religion that makes large-scale claims and fails to live up to those claims must be considered unsatisfactory. Moreover, it is important that enough time elapse so that the results can be established on a stronger basis. Some things appear to work for a season but in the long pull they fade and fail. Christianity meets the pragmatic test in such a fashion that any disinterested observer would have to be impressed with its record over two thousand years.

God Himself in Scripture employed the pragmatic method, so that men would know they were not deceived or that they were falling for something that was untrue or illicit or fraudulent. Father Abraham was given outward confirming evidence that his faith in the God who had spoken to him was not mistaken. He prepared an animal sacrifice and when it had been cut in two and darkness had come "a smoking fire pot and a flaming torch passed between these pieces." And God spoke His word to Abraham in covenant promise.

Jesus Himself willingly turned to the pragmatic to establish before men the fact that He was what He claimed to be. He said He was the Son of God. And when this statement was questioned, Jesus replied to His critics, "Even though you do not believe me [that is, His words], believe the works, that you may know and understand that the Father is in me and I am in the Father" (John 10:38). The miracles performed by Jesus were outward confirming signs, pragmatic evidence, that He was indeed the Redeemer.

Everywhere, Scripture invites men to come to Jesus Christ with the promise that when they do they shall have evidences so convincing that they will be satisfied. These evidences consist in two things. The first is the assurance wrought in their hearts that they have been justified before God. The second is the new birth, or regeneration, by which they actually become new creations in Christ Jesus. There is the changed life that proves to the person whose life is changed, and to those outside who see the transformed life, that what the Bible promises it delivers.

For two thousand years, the Church of Jesus Christ has manifested before the eyes of an unbelieving world that Jesus Christ does make a difference. Because of Him, thousands of people have lived noble lives. Tens of thousands of people have willingly suffered martyrdom by burning, by torture, and by the axe. Children and grandchildren have followed the faith of their fathers and continued their witness. James Taylor in Taiwan is the great-great-grandson of J. Hudson Taylor, who founded the China Inland Mission, now known as the Overseas Missionary Fellowship. And his children are following in his, and in his forebears, steps.

Jesus said, "Come unto me, and I will give you rest." This has proved to be true in millions of lives, and is true today. Evangelistic crusades like those conducted by Billy Graham have brought together masses of people around the world. And the continuing testimony of the masses who have assembled has been to the efficacy of the Christian faith. Multiplied thousands of people have found Christ as Savior in these crusades and have gone forth to lead lives of commitment to Jesus Christ. Local congregations of believers around the globe have gathered Sunday after Sunday to break the bread of the divine Presence, drink of the cup of His crucifixion, and then have sent forth from their midst missionaries who have sailed the high seas and crossed the highest mountains to share their faith with those who have never heard.

There is no Christian who is unable to testify that God answers prayer. There is today, as there has been through the ages, the witness of broken bodies that have been healed, and scarred and dirty souls that have been cleansed.

Doubters may spurn this sort of witness and discount the testimony of these millions of people who have found Jesus to be the answer to life's great needs. The Christian answer to every sceptic and critic is this: Try it. You will be convinced, once you have entered into a relationship with Jesus, for it will show you pragmatically that He is no disappointment to those who venture forth in faith.

The Witness of the Church Through the Reformation

We have spoken of some of the reasons why we believe the Bible is to be trusted in all of its parts. Would it not be peculiar if, believing the Bible to be true, we found that no one through the centuries held to this viewpoint? We surely would want to know why we should then believe what no one had believed through the years. But it leads to a second question no less important, one that turns the issue in the opposite direction. If the Church through the ages believed the Bible to be altogether true, why, then, are there those today who assault a view held so long by the Church? So we must look at the witness of the Church and believers through the ages, with respect to their convictions about the Bible's truthfulness.

The Jewish View of the Old Testament

The first place to start is not after Pentecost. Rather, we must ask what the Jews of Jesus' day believed about the Old Testament Scripture. When we do this, we quickly discover that they held the highest view of it. This has been acknowledged even by modern liberals who dissent from that view. The first series of these testimonies come from the pens of people who either were not Christians, or who have been known as liberal scholars. Yet the testimony of all is to the effect that the people of Jesus' day held a very high view of the Old Testament.

Josephus

Perhaps we should start with the famed Josephus, the ancient Jewish historian. George Duncan Barry, who composed a landmark book on the subject of inerrancy in the history of the Church, says that Josephus held a very high view of the Old Testament. He wrote, "In Josephus we are dealing...with an author who wrote more especially for Gentile readers. The high estimate which Josephus formed of the Sacred Books coincides closely with that of Philo: his reverence for them is based on his belief that their authors wrote under the influence of the Divine Spirit." "In speaking of Moses, Josephus describes him as a prophet in so exalted a sense that his words are to be regarded as the words of God Himself. Of Isaiah he says that he was a prophet confessedly divine, and unhesitatingly avers that all the prophecies of Isaiah and of the twelve Minor Prophets have been literally fulfilled; and thereby the Divine authority of the writers has been vindicated beyond all suspicion." "The fullest statement of the views held by Josephus of the authority and inspiration of the Bible is to be found in a celebrated passage of his treatise, *Contra Apionem,*...'There is no discrepancy in the facts recorded.'...'The prophets learnt their message "by reason of the inspiration they received from God" ': they compiled accurately the history of their own time." "It is impossible to conceive language which could assign a higher authority to the Bible than that which he used" (George Duncan Barry, THE INSPIRATION AND AUTHORITY OF HOLY SCRIPTURE, A STUDY IN THE LITERATURE OF THE FIRST FIVE CENTURIES [New York, Macmillan, 1919], pp. 19ff.).

Rudolph Bultmann

Professor Bultmann, assessed by many as one of the great New Testament scholars, and himself the father of modern demythologization by which he nullified Scripture, had this to say:

Jesus agreed always with the scribes of his time in accepting without question the authority of the (Old Testament) Law. When he was asked by the rich man, "What must I do to inherit eternal life," he answered, "You know the commandments," and he repeated the well-known Old Testament Decalogue... Jesus did not attack the Law but assumed its authority and interpreted it...And from this time (after Jesus' day when Paul and others preached) came the well-known words, which Jesus surely cannot have said: "Do not suppose that I have come to destroy but to fulfill. I tell you truly, until heaven and earth vanish, no letter nor point can vanish from the Law until all is fulfilled. Whoever erases one of the smallest commandments and so teaches others shall be called least in the Kingdom of Heaven. But whoever keeps it and teaches it shall be called great in the Kingdom of Heaven (Matthew 5:17-19)" (*Jesus and the Word* [New York: Scribner's 1934], p. 61).

Several points in this statement are noteworthy. Bultmann says the belief of the scribes in Jesus' day was exactly the same as the view of Jesus. And while he does not think that Jesus really spoke some of the words attributed to Him, yet he acknowledged that the words indicate the highest possible view of the trustworthiness of the Bible.

Professor F.C. Grant

Union Theological Seminary (New York) professor F.C. Grant has left us an excellent testimony that the writers of the New Testament, most of them Jews of Jesus' day, believed as Jesus did in the infallibility of the Old Testament. He penned these words:

The passage quoted from Second Timothy is the most explicit statement of the doctrine of biblical inspiration to be found in the New Testament. But its view of inspiration is not more advanced than that of any other part of the volume, as an examination of the passages cited in a concordance (s.v. "scripture" and "written") will show. Everywhere it is taken for granted that what is written in Scripture is the work of divine inspiration, and is therefore trustworthy, infallible, and inerrant. The Scripture must be "fulfilled" (Luke 22:37). What was written there was "written for our instruction" (Romans 15:4; 1 Corinthians 10:11). What is described or related in the Old Testament is unquestionably true. No New Testament writer would dream of questioning a statement contained in the Old Testament, though the exact manner or mode of its inspiration is nowhere explicitly stated (*An Introduction to New Testament Thought* [New York: Abingdon Cokesbury, 1950], p. 75).

Professor Grant, when he wrote these words, was in no way affirming personal belief in biblical infallibility. But he did affirm that it was taught and believed by Jesus, and the writers of the New Testament. Dr. Grant was certainly honest in that he nowhere suggests that the writers of the New Testament did not believe in the total trustworthiness of the Old Testament.

Professors Cadbury, Harnack, and Knox

Dr. Kenneth Kantzer, dean of the Trinity Evangelical Divinity School and himself a Ph.D from Harvard and an evangelical, made an observation about three well-known scholars who denied biblical infallibility but who, at the same time, admitted that the view they denied was the view taught and believed by the Jews, Jesus, and the Apostles:

H.J. Cadbury, Harvard professor and one of the more extreme New Testament critics of the last generation, once declared that he was far more sure as a mere historical fact that Jesus held to the common Jewish view of an infallible Bible than that Jesus believed in His own messiahship. Adolph Harnack, greatest church historian of modern times, insists that Christ was one with His apostles, the Jews, and the entire early Church, in complete commitment to the infallible authority of the Bible. John Knox, author of what is perhaps the most highly regarded recent life of Christ, states that there can be no question that this view of the Bible was taught by our Lord himself (Harold Lindsell, ed., *The Church's Worldwide Mission* [Waco: Word, 1966], p. 31).

The Early Church Fathers

George Duncan Barry, himself no believer in inerrancy, said this of the early church fathers:

The fact that for fifteen centuries no attempt was made to formulate a definition of the doctrine of inspiration of the Bible, testifies to the universal belief of the Church that the Scriptures were the handiwork of the Holy Ghost...It was, to our modern judgment, a mechanical and erroneous view of inspiration that was accepted and taught by the Church of the first centuries, seeing that it ruled out all possibility of error in matters either of history or of doctrine. Men expressed their belief in the inspiration and authority of the Bible in language which startles us by its strange want of reserve. The Scriptures were regarded as writings of the Holy Spirit, no room at all being left for the play of the human agent in the Divine Hands. The writers were used by Him as a workman uses his tools; in a word, the Books, the actual words, rather than the writers, were inspired (Barry, *op. cit.,* p. 10).

Barry's statement is helpful for several reasons. First, he shows that the early church fathers did believe in an inerrant Bible. And the absence of any evidence to show that there were important fathers who held to an errant Scripture makes the case foolproof. Second, his witness is helpful because he himself does not hold the view that he says the church fathers held. The testimony of the opposition is, in some ways, even more important than the testimony of those who favor inerrancy. Third, he indicates that the view of the early fathers

about the divine activity in inscripturation was so high that one is left
with the distinct impression that the "words, rather than the writers,
were inspired." This means that the early fathers believed in verbal
inspiration and some of them, perhaps, even in dictation. There may
have been differences of opinion about how the Bible was given, but
there was no difference of opinion that once it was given the product
was wholly without error from beginning to end.

Augustine

For the sake of brevity, we need not quote the numerous references from the church fathers to demonstrate what scholars have had
to admit--that they taught the doctrine of biblical infallibility. But it
will help us if mention is made of one of the truly great fathers of the
Church, Augustine. He is of more than passing interest, because of
the tremendous influence his writings had on John Calvin. In THE
INSTITUTES OF THE CHRISTIAN RELIGION, Calvin quotes
more from Augustine than from any other writer apart from the
Bible itself. Augustine's attitude and understanding of biblical inerrancy is significant. "The Faith will totter if the authority of the
Holy Scriptures loses its hold on men. We must surrender ourselves
to the authority of Holy Scripture, for it can neither mislead nor be
misled." "The question," says Barry, " 'Why Christ Himself did
not write any Book' is answered by Augustine in these remarkable
words. 'His members gave out the knowledge which they had received *through the dictation of the Head*; whatever He willed us to
read concerning His own words and acts, He bade them write, as
though they were His own very words. More unguardedly still,
Augustine teaches that we see in the Gospels the very Hand of the
Lord which He wore in His own Body...There are no contradictions
of each other's writings in the Books of the Four Evangelists. 'We
must demonstrate that the Four Sacred writers are not at variance
with each other. For our opponents...frequently maintain that discrepancies are found in the Evangelists'...Freely do I admit to you,
my friend, that I have learnt to ascribe to those Books which are of
Canonical rank, and only to them, such reverence and honour, that I
firmly believe that no single error due to the author is found in any
one of them. And when I am confronted in these Books with anything that seems to be at variance with truth, I do not hesitate to put
it down either to the use of an incorrect text, or to the failure of a
commentator rightly to explain the words, or to my own mistaken
understanding of the passage" (Barry, *op. cit.,* pp. 140ff).

Augustine went further than a simple belief in an inerrant Bible.
He argued strongly about the consequences of undermining that

viewpoint. In one of his letters to Jerome, he said that once you admit a single error in the Bible you open the door to a floodtide of unbelief. "For it seems to me that most disastrous consequences must follow upon our believing that anything false is found in the sacred books: that is to say, that the men by whom the Scripture has been given to us, and committed to writing, did put down in these books anything false. It is one question whether it may be at any time the duty of a good man to deceive; but it is another question whether it can have been the duty of a writer of Holy Scripture to deceive: nay, it is not another question--it is no question at all. For if you once admit into such a high sanctuary of authority one false statement as made in the way of duty, there will not be left a single sentence of those books which, if appearing to any one difficult in practice or hard to believe, may not by the same fatal rule be explained away, as a statement in which, intentionally, and under a sense of duty, the author declared what was not true...

"For my part, I would devote all the strength which the Lord grants me, to show that every one of those texts which are wont to be quoted in defence of the expediency of falsehood ought to be otherwise understood, in order than everywhere the sure truth of these passages themselves may be consistently maintained. For as statements adduced in evidence must not be false, neither ought they to favour falsehood. This, however, I leave to your own judgment. For if you apply more thorough attention to the passage, perhaps you will see it much more readily than I have done. To this more careful study that piety will move you, by which you discern that the authority of the divine Scriptures becomes unsettled (so that every one may believe what he wishes, and reject what he does not wish) if this be once admitted, that the men by whom these things have been delivered unto us, could in their writings state some things which were not true, from considerations of duty; unless, perchance, you propose to furnish us with certain rules by which we may know when a falsehood might or might not become a duty. If this can be done, I beg you to set forth these rules with reasonings which may be neither equivocal nor precarious" (*A Select Library of the Nicene and Post-Nicene Fathers of the Christian Church,* First Series, Vol. I, [New York: The Christian Literature Company, 1892], pp. 252,253).

The Catholic Church

In the early history of the Christian Church, tensions arose between the eastern and western branches that finally led to schism. The eastern establishment was centered in Constantinople; the western or Latin establishment had Rome for its center. The church

of Rome became the ascendant branch of the formerly united
church, and its history has been part and parcel of western Christen-
dom. Both branches of the church, eastern and western, held to an
infallible Scripture. But the Church of Rome is of more interest to
us, since it was the church dynamically connected with European
Christianity and was locked in a great struggle with men like Calvin
and Luther in the Reformation. The Roman Catholic or Latin
Church held a very high view of the Bible through the centuries. It is
true that the Church of Rome did add tradition as a source of religious knowledge; and this became a driving wedge that helped to
precipitate the struggle with Martin Luther, who insisted on the
principle of *sola scriptura,* i.e., the Bible alone as the source of our
religious knowledge.

We need only take a casual look at almost any Catholic dictionary or encyclopedia to confirm the fact that for more than a thousand years that church, formally, accepted and taught that the Bible
is inerrant in all of its parts. There were two views the Roman church
repudiated: one was the view that the Holy Spirit "secured the writers from error only in matters of faith and morals." This is one of
the views that is being advanced in various forms today. But it is not
a new view. It has simply surfaced again, or has been advocated in
slightly different forms. The *Catholic Dictionary* (New York: Addis
and Arnold, 1884, p. 450) says that in 1685, Holden in his work,
Analysis Fidei, defended the limited inerrancy standpoint but got
nowhere. The other view that the Roman church repudiated was
mechanical dictation. For some reason, they associated that view
with the term *verbal inspiration* and in their differences with Protestants said that this view found wide acceptance among the older
Protestant theologians. Suarez (*De Fide,* disp. 5, & 3. n. 3, 5) maintained it is "enough to believe that the Holy Spirit 'specially assisted
him (the author of the inspired book, while writing) and kept him
from all error and falsehood, and from all words which were not ex-
pedient.' " The same article says that Ballermin's *De Verbo Dei*, lib.
v. 15; Melchoir Canus, *De. Loc. Theolog.* lib. ii. cc 17 et 18, say the
same thing.

The dictionary also says that "if Holden's theory sins against
the received teaching and tradition (which it did), most certainly that
of verbal inspiration as it has just been explained (the authors of the
Biblical books were no more than scribes who wrote down the words
which the Holy Spirit dictated) sins against the most patent facts.
Evidently the style and method of the sacred writers is coloured
throughout by their own individuality, and the differences in
thought and language between Isaiah and Ezechiel (*sic*) are utterly

inexplicable if we regard them as passive agents under a mechanical inspiration. St. Augustine in well known words formulises the prevailing belief of the Church without falling into the exaggerations of the theory that inspiration is mechanical" (then follows the statement by Augustine quoted above).

What is important to note in this connection is that there are no evangelical scholars who hold to mechanical dictation, although it is true that those who hold to biblical inerrancy do believe in verbal inspiration in the sense that inspiration extends to the words, not just to the thoughts or ideas, and yet the writers kept their own styles and individuality. It is significant also that the Catholic church accepted Augustine's classic statement and used it in principle in the consecration of bishops. In the "Symbol of Faith," approved by Leo IX-- and used in the consecration of bishops--God is affirmed to be the " 'one author' of the Old and the New Testaments."

The Catholic Encyclopedia (N.Y., Robert Appleton, Vol. 2, 1907, p. 543) makes this statement about the Bible:

> The Bible...is the word of God...The inerrancy of the Bible follows as a consequence of the Divine authorship. Wherever the sacred writer makes a statement as his own, the statement is the word of God and infallibly true, whatever the subject matter of the statement.

This appraisal of the church's view is fully in agreement with that of *The Catholic Dictionary* and differs from the next encyclopedic reference at one point: these reference works so far not only define biblical infallibility but assent to it. The following reference agrees that inerrancy has been the view of the church through the ages, but reveals the new fact that many in the Roman or Latin church no longer hold to what has been the view of the church until quite recently.

The latest *New Catholic Encyclopedia* (New York: McGraw, 1967, Vol. II, p. 384) contains a statement about inerrancy, "The inerrancy of Scripture has been the constant teaching of the Fathers, the theologians, and recent Popes in their encyclicals on Biblical studies (Leo XIII, Ench Bibl 124-131; Benedict XV, Ench Bibl 453-461; Pius XII, Ench Bibl 560). It is nonetheless obvious that many biblical statements are simply not true when judged according to modern knowledge of science and history. The earth is not stationary (cf. Ecclesiastes 1:4); Darius the Mede did not succeed Belsassar (cf. Daniel 5:30-6:1)." What the Encyclopedia is saying is patent to all. The church has *always* (via Fathers, theologians, the popes) taught biblical inerrancy. Some no longer believe it, despite the fact that it has been the church's viewpoint for centuries. The so-called errors pointed to are the same kinds of errors alluded to by modern evangelicals as the reason for supporting limited inerrancy, and in some cases not even that.

The Reformers

So we now come to the age of the Reformers, to see what their witness to Scripture is and what they believed and taught. It would be a mistake to suppose that the Reformers formulated a viewpoint such as those expressed by the early ecumenical councils when they were dealing with Christology. It must be remembered that the Reformers spent their time talking about the issues that were important in the struggle against the Roman church. Since the Roman church held to a view of Scripture that was no different from that held by the Reformers, there was no real problem. The problem came from adding to Scripture, and was not concerned with whether Scripture could be trusted; it was about interpretation, not inerrancy. The role of the church as the unerring interpreter of Scripture over against the universal priesthood of all believers was important; and the Reformers believed that the church could err in interpretation.

Martin Luther

We come first to Martin Luther. Luther believed and taught that the Bible was infallibly true in all its parts. Of that there can be no doubt. But it is useless to look in his writings for a developed thesis to support biblical inerrancy. He believed it; it was not in dispute; he wrote all of his works based on his belief that the Bible was true. But he does leave us with much evidence as to his confidence in the truth of Scripture.

Luther quoted from Augustine's letter to Jerome in which he wrote, "This I have learned to do: to hold only those books which are called the Holy Scriptures in such honor that I finally believe that not one of the holy writers ever erred." Luther endorsed this view of Augustine and himself stated, "The Scriptures *cannot* err" (XIX:1073). "It is certain that Scripture cannot disagree with itself" (XX:798). "It is impossible that Scripture should contradict itself, only that is so appears to the senseless and obstinate hypocrites" (IX:356). "One little point of doctrine means more than heaven and earth, and therefore we cannot suffer to have the least jot thereof violated" (IX:650). "For it is established by God's Word that God does not lie, nor does His Word lie" (XX:798).

When Luther found an apparent discrepancy with respect to chronology, he refused to side with "those rash men who in the case of a Bible difficulty are not afraid to say that Scripture is evidently wrong. I conclude the matter with a humble confession of my ignorance, for it is only the Holy Ghost who knows and understands everything" (1:721). (Theodore Engelder, *Scripture Cannot Be Broken* [St. Louis: Concordia, 1944], quotes from Luther's work.)

J. Theodore Mueller in his book, *Luther and the Bible,* (pp. 99,103) says that "Luther unfailingly asserts the inerrancy of Scripture over against the errancy of human historians and scientists. He writes, 'The Scriptures have never erred...' " He also argues that the Lutheran "Dr. Reu champions the following theses, namely, that Scripture was the sole authority of Luther; that Luther's preface to the Epistle of James does not prove a different attitude; that Scripture remained Luther's sole authority of the Christian faith till the end of his life; that Luther never admitted any error in Scripture; that Luther considered even those parts of the Bible that do not concern our salvation as inerrant; that Luther ascribed absolute inerrancy to the original drafts of the Bible and that Luther did not teach a mechanical theory of inspiration. Luther indeed believed in verbal and plenary inspiration but not in a mechanical diction theory." Mueller also quotes the Lutheran Dr. H. Echternach approvingly, " 'The infallibility of Scripture was the consensus of the Church, irrespective of denominational lines, until long after 1700 A.D.' "

Robert Preus (*The Inspiration of Scripture, A Study of the Theology of the Seventeenth Century Lutheran Dogmaticians* [London, 1955], pp. 58,66,67) wrote about the Lutheran Quenstadt who followed in Luther's footsteps. Of all the Lutherans of that era, perhaps none excelled Quenstadt, who has been charged with holding to a mechanical dictation view of inspiration. We must remember again that whether one holds to this or to some other view of *how* inerrancy came about, the fact remains that the end process, by whichever method one chooses, is an inerrant Scripture. But Quenstadt was hardly guilty of all the allegations leveled against him. Preus points out that Quenstadt believed Scripture was not brought into being monergistically (i.c., by God or by man alone). He quotes Quenstadt, " 'We must distinguish between those who have been snatched away and are in a trance and do not know what they are doing and saying and between the apostles whom the Holy Spirit activated in such a way that they understood those things which they were speaking and writing.' " Preus claims that "the mechanical idea of inspiration was not only foreign to the dogmaticians, it was loudly and consciously condemned by them. They were opposed to every conception of inspiration which would degrade the writers to the status of inanimate objects which neither thought nor felt in the act of writing but to which God imparted revelation as one might pour water into a pail."

Quenstadt, says Preus, "true to form, states the orthodox position in a manner which defies misunderstanding. He says, 'The holy
canonical Scriptures in their original text are the infallible truth and
free from every error, that is to say, in the sacred canonical Scriptures there is no lie, no deceit, no error, even the slightest, either in
content or words, but every single word which is handed down in the
Scriptures is most true, whether it pertains to doctrine, ethics,
history, chronology, typography, or onomastic; and no ignorance,
lack of understanding, forgetfulness or lapse of memory can be attributed to the amanuenses of the Holy Spirit in their writing of Holy
Scriptures' " (*Ibid.*, p. 77).

One aspect of Luther's approach to the Word of God requires
elaboration. Currently, a number of Lutherans keep pointing out the
fact that Luther, when using the term "the Word of God," did not
have Scripture in mind, but Jesus Christ. Pelikan of Yale has
stressed this, as have those who are opposed to biblical inerrancy.
Historically, it is true that Luther used the term "the Word of God"
when he had Jesus Christ in mind, and he did this frequently. But it
would be incorrect to say that he did this *all* the time. Moreover,
there are enough evidences available to prove conclusively that Luther
also used the term "the Word of God" to mean Scripture. He also
used the word *Scripture,* and there are sufficient evidences to show
that he regarded Scripture as inerrant. Clearly, Luther knew there
are two "Words of God," the Word of God incarnate and the Word
of God written, and he held both of them to be completely trustworthy. So no one need get hung up on this issue, nor spend time
arguing whether on this occasion or that Luther meant Jesus Christ
or the Scripture when he spoke of "the Word of God."

John Calvin

What can be said of Luther can be said also of John Calvin. He
held the Scriptures in the highest esteem and believed them to be infallible in all their parts. Perhaps the best modern acknowledgement
of Calvin's convictions about Scripture comes from the pen of Edward A. Dowey, Jr., who was the chief architect of the United Presbyterian's *New Confession*. His doctoral dissertation covered this
question. He says of Calvin that we owe their (the apostles' and
prophets') writings in Scripture "the same reverence which we owe
to God, because it has proceeded from him alone and has nothing
human mixed in...We ought to embrace with mild docility, and without exception, whatever is delivered in the Holy Scriptures. For
Scripture is the school of the Holy Spirit in which as nothing useful
and necessary is omitted, so nothing is taught which is not profitable

to know" (*The Knowledge of God in Calvin's Theology* [New York: Columbia, 1952], p. 91).

Dowey says that when Calvin "does admit an undeniable error of grammar or of fact, without exception he attributes it to copyists, never to the inspired writer. There is no hint anywhere in Calvin's writings that the original text contained any flaws at all" (*Ibid.*, p. 100). It is of more than just passing interest to note here that critics like Charles Augustus Briggs, of whom more shall be said later, constantly criticized Benjamin Warfield as the inventor of the notion that inerrancy belongs to the autographs. He speaks of this as a late contribution brought about by an inability to demonstrate the infallibility of the copies. But Dowey here makes it plain that Calvin, where he does find a difficulty, lays it to a copyist's error, and this can mean only that Calvin regarded the autographs as infallible.

According to Dowey, "Neither in these places nor anywhere else does Calvin discuss in detail the method by which the Scripture was preserved. This leaves an interesting hiatus in his doctrine. It is interesting precisely because it is always to the text before him, never to the original text of Scripture, that Calvin attributes such errors as his exegesis discovers" (*Ibid.*, p. 103). "To Calvin the theologian an error in Scripture is unthinkable. Hence the endless harmonizing, the explaining and interpreting of passages that seem to contradict or to be inaccurate" (*Ibid.*, p. 104). "If he [Calvin] betrays his position at all, it is apparently in assuming *a priori* that no errors can be allowed to reflect upon the inerrancy of the original documents" (*Ibid.*, p. 105). Here are Calvin's own words, "For if we consider how slippery is the human mind...how prone to all kinds of error...we can perceive how necessary is such a repository of heavenly doctrine, that it will neither perish by forgetfulness, nor vanish in error, nor be corrupted by the audacity of men" (*Ibid.*, p. 105). "The question of authority supplies the dominant motif in Calvin's doctrine of Biblical authority, as well as his doctrine of faith in general. No hearsay about God can be the foundation of Christian assurance...The divine origin of Scripture, the fact that it has come 'from heaven' is that to which the Spirit gives witness, and this transfers authority from me to God" (*Ibid.*, p. 109).

Does Calvin's belief in biblical inerrancy mean he held that the mode of inspiration was by dictation? Dowey went into this question also, for there were evidences in Calvin's writings that might lead to such a conclusion. He says, "We must now consider whether Calvin's teaching about inspiration as so far presented requires the interpretation that Calvin held a mechanical or literal dictation theory of the writing of the Bible. He incontrovertibly did mean literal interpretation in his description of Jeremiah's inspiration, cited above (*Supra.,* pp. 92f). His emphasis as seen throughout our study of the miraculous accompaniments of inspiration upon the transmission of the message, in my opinion, add weight to the claim that he conceived the Scriptures as literally dictated by God...Most of what today are recognized as idiosyncrasies in style and even mistakes in the text are attributed to the purposes of the Holy Spirit. To this end, the principle of accommodation is for Calvin a common exegetical device for explaining away irregularities that might otherwise, with a less rigorous view of the perfection of the text, be simply attributed to inaccuracies. When he does admit an undeniable error of grammar or of fact, without exception he attributes it to copyists, never to the inspired writer (*Infra.,* pp. 104f.). There is no hint anywhere in Calvin's writings that the original text contained any flaws at all" (*Ibid.,* p. 99).

Dowey then asserts that "R. Seeberg, O. Ritschl, and A.M. Hunter...attribute unambiguously a diction theory to Calvin. These are closer to the truth, but probably the solution of Warfield, curious as it appears at first glance, is the best formulation for doing justice to a certain lack of clarity or variation in Calvin himself. Concerning 'dictation,' Warfield comments, 'It is not unfair to urge, however, that this language is figurative and that what Calvin has in mind, is, not to insist that the mode of inspiration was dictation, but that the result of inspiration is as if it were by dictation, viz., the production of a pure word of God free from all human admixtures...The important thing to realize is that according to Calvin the Scriptures were so given that--whether by "literal" or "figurative" dictation--the result was a series of documents errorless in their original form' " (*Ibid.,* p. 101,102).

One item in the testimony of John Calvin should be explained. A number of opponents of biblical inerrancy have attributed to Calvin the opinion that he rejected the Petrine authorship of 2 Peter. This is important because modern critics not only claim that this Epistle was not written by Peter; they also claim that it is a second-century, not a first-century, product. The problem of Petrine authorship, it should be stated, is not a modern one. It has existed in the church for centuries. Calvin was involved in this, too. Of 2 Peter he says in his commentary on that book:

> If it is received as canonical, we must admit that Peter is the author, not only because it bears his name, but also because he testifies that he lived with Christ. It would have been a fiction unworthy of a minister of Christ to pretend to be another personality. Therefore I conclude that if the epistle is trustworthy it

has come from Peter; not that he wrote it himself, but that one of his disciples composed by his command what the necessity of the times demanded. It is probable that at the time he was very old; he says he is near to death, and it could be that at the request of the godly he allowed this testament of his mind to be signed and sealed just before his death, because it might have some force after he was dead to encourage the good and repress the wicked. Certainly since the majesty of the Spirit of Christ expresses itself in all parts of the epistle, I have a dread of repudiating it, even though I do not recognize in it the genuine language of Peter. Since there is no agreement as to the author, I shall allow myself to use the name of Peter or the apostle indiscriminately (John Calvin, *The Epistle of Paul the Apostle to the Hebrews, and the First and Second Epistles of St. Peter* [Grand Rapids: Eerdmans, 1957], p. 325).

From Calvin's own statement, we should note several things. First, he acknowledged that if one accepts 2 Peter as canonical it must be admitted that Peter is the author, simply because the Epistle so claims. Calvin would be at variance with modern critics who advocate the viewpoint that someone used Peter's name long after his death and that this device is acceptable. Calvin says no! Moreover, he makes it plain that 2 Peter was written during Peter's lifetime. He refuses to date it in another century even as he refuses to let it come from a forger who has used Peter's name. It is true, on the other hand, that Calvin had trouble with the language of 2 Peter, and it was this that occasioned his suggestion that perhaps the Epistle was written by an amanuensis under the supervision of the aged apostle, in which case it was a genuine product of the apostle. Calvin does not hesitate to say that, allowing for the possibility that Peter had someone write it under his supervision and control, he uses the name of Peter or the apostle as the author indiscriminately. Thus the faith of Calvin in the inerrancy of Scripture overcame his scholar's questions and Peter remained for him the true author of the Epistle that bears his name.

Anyone who reads Calvin and Luther and compares them with modern writers who deny biblical infallibility cannot fail to note the difference between the attitude of the Reformers and that of the modern objectors to infallibility. The latter unfailingly seek to denigrate Scripture, to humanize it, to swallow a camel and strain out a gnat. The Reformers did not react in this way. Their attitude toward the Word of God was one of reverence, humility, and positive acceptance of it as both authoritative and infallible.

Summary

What conclusions can we draw from what has been said thus far? Certainly, it is apparent that the Jews of Jesus' day, the Lord Jesus Himself, and the apostles all believed that the Old Testament was free from error. They believed it in all of its parts. Once the New Testament was added to the Old, we have the witness of the fathers across the centuries. And their virtually universal witness has been that of undiluted faith in Scripture. This was true not only of the fathers but of the organized church. The Latin church as well as the Eastern church held to biblical infallibility. The Reformation brought no change either to the basic view of the Catholic church about the Bible or of the Reformers. They clung tenaciously to what the Jews, Jesus, the apostles, and the fathers believed and propagated.

Now we must ask ourselves what the situation has been since the Reformation. This is important because most of the Protestant denominations that trace their history back to the Reformation, or before the Reformation to some of the reforming groups that existed before Luther and Calvin fathered the Lutheran and the Reformed churches, have made statements and commitments about the Bible. We turn our attention to the witness of the churches and Christians since the Reformation.

The Church's Testimony Since the Reformation

At the outset, we should consider a statement made by Kirsop Lake, an eminent New Testament scholar and a professor at the University of Chicago. This is what he wrote:

It is a mistake often made by educated persons who happen to have but little knowledge of historical theology, to suppose that fundamentalism is a new and strange form of thought. It is nothing of the kind; it is the partial and uneducated survival of a theology which was once universally held by all Christians. How many were there, for instance, in Christian churches in the eighteenth century who doubted the infallible inspiration of all Scripture? A few, perhaps, but very few. No, the fundamentalist may be wrong; I think that he is. But it is we who have departed from the tradition, not he, and I am sorry for the fate of anyone who tries to argue with a fundamentalist on the basis of authority. The Bible and the *corpus theologicum* of the Church is on the fundamentalist side (*The Religion of Yesterday and Tomorrow* [Boston: Houghton, 1926], p. 61.

Professor Lake's testimony, written at the height of the Modernist-Fundamentalist controversy, helps us understand the situation in several ways. First, he acknowledges that those who hold to an inerrant Bible have the witness of the Bible itself on their side. Secondly, he correctly affirms that until the eighteenth century there were few people who denied biblical infallibility. But at the same time, he is aware of the fact that since the eighteenth century a battle has been raging over a question the Church and Christians had answered to their satisfaction for many centuries. In other words, the current denial by many of the complete trustworthiness of the Bible is a contemporary and recent phenomenon and runs counter to the established view of the Church.

We must remember that through the ages conflicts have raged about important aspects of God's revelation to men. This should occasion no surprise, for the Church has been wracked by troubles from its inception. Shortly after Pentecost, the apostles had to deal with Ananias and Sapphira who bore false witness in an effort to gain applause by selling property and giving the money for the poor. But they held back part of the proceeds. The Spirit of God dealt justly with them, and they died for their wickedness. Moreover, the Grecians murmured against the Hebrews "because their widows were neglected in the daily ministration" (Acts 6:1). The apostles established the office of deacon so they could continue their particular ministry without letup while others cared for the more mundane matters of life. The apostle Paul later encountered theological difficulty with the Judaizers. Paul and Peter differed over keeping some of the Old Testament prohibitions in an age of grace. John wrote about gnostics who claimed that Jesus had not really come in the flesh; He only *seemed* to have a human body.

The early church had to consider serious problems about the person of Jesus. Eventually these were resolved. The heresy of Arius, who taught that Jesus was a created being, was settled by affirming that there never was a time when the second person of the Holy Trinity was not. And other matters were decided. Jesus was declared to be one person over against Nestorius, and that He had a perfectly divine and a perfectly human nature in that one person. It was also affirmed that the incarnate Word had a divine and a human will.

Later on, the Church wrestled with questions having to do with the nature of man. The so-called anthropological (*anthropos* means man) problems were worked out. In the time of the Reformation, the great questions were, "Are men saved by faith plus works?" and, "Is righteousness infused or imputed?" It was not until the eighteenth century that the question, "Is the Bible trustworthy in all of its parts?" dominated the scene. From the eighteenth century until this moment, the Church has wrestled with this problem. Basically, the Modernist-Fundamentalist controversy revolved around this issue. Neo-orthodoxy intimately associated with the name of Karl Barth, came into the picture after World War I. Basically, neo-orthodoxy was, and is still, asking whether the Bible is the Word of

God or becomes the Word of God in a confrontation experience. The Barthian view was and is in direct conflict with the orthodox view of the Bible through the ages.

The Various Witnesses

With this brief summary in mind, we turn our attention to the witness of the various denominations to the trustworthiness of the Bible, as well as the witness of key believers since the days of the Reformation.

The Westminster Confession of Faith

Among the confessions of faith in the Reformed tradition, none ever written is superior to the Westminster Confession in scope, clarity, and precision. Chapter 1 sets forth the doctrine of Scripture. It is called "the only infallible rule of faith and practice." From this, some have argued that the Westminster Confession in effect limited inerrancy to matters of faith and practice, excluding matters having to do with history, science, and cosmology.

The error of this may be seen when two facts are taken into account. One is the entire statement on Scripture, which includes two phrases that destroy the limited inerrancy notion. The Confession speaks of "the entire perfection" of Scripture and acknowledges the "consent of all the parts." These portions of the definition rule out the notion of limited inerrancy.

But more than that, the history of the times must be taken into account. We have noted that during the Reformation period biblical infallibility was a tenet accepted by both the Roman Catholic Church and the Reformers. It was not central to the dispute that occasioned the rupture. Had it been, the Reformers would have pinpointed the issue; and the canons of the Council of Trent, in which the Roman Catholics answered the Reformers, would have included a counterblast. At the time the Westminster Confession was adopted, there was no serious challenge to the view of biblical infallibility, and the Confession did not speak to the issue the way it undoubtedly would have had there been such a difference of opinion.

So far as the United States is concerned, the Westminster Confession of Faith had its most avid proponents in Princeton Theological Seminary, the oldest and most venerable seminary among Presbyterians. Founded in 1812, it taught its students consistently for more than a hundred years that the Bible is free from error. Archibald Alexander was the first professor, and he made the works of Francis Turretin central to the curriculum. Turretin held the highest view of biblical authority and infallibility. For more than half a century, the works of Turretin were taught at the Seminary. Charles Hodge, who replaced Professor Alexander, authored his own *Systematic Theology,* a massive three-volume work that is still in print today. In 1872, this work supplanted that of Turretin as the standard text in theology at Princeton.

Charles Hodge taught that the Bible is free from all error whether of doctrine, fact, or precept (*Systematic Theology* [N.Y., Scribner], Vol. I, p. 152). Archibald Alexander Hodge and Benjamin B. Warfield continued the tradition, and in their conflict with Charles Augustus Briggs stoutly defended inerrancy. Dr. Warfield said that "a proved error in Scripture contradicts not only our doctrine, but the Scripture claims and, therefore, its inspiration in making those claims" (*The Presbyterian Review,* April, 1881, p. 238). The General Assembly of the Presbyterian Church in 1893 and again in 1924 upheld the theological position of Hodge and Warfield on the inerrancy of the autographs of the Bible.

It was not until after 1930 that the old Princeton theology gave way to the new theology of an errant Bible. This was expressed by one notable teacher in these words, "Few intelligent Christians can still hold to the idea that the Bible is an infallible Book, that it contains no linguistic errors, no historical discrepancies, no antiquated scientific assumptions, not even bad ethical standards. Historical investigation and literary criticism have taken the magic out of the Bible, and have made it a composite human book, written by many hands in different ages. The existence of thousands of variations of texts makes it impossible to hold the doctrine of a book verbally infallible. Some might claim for the original copies of the Bible an infallible character, but this view only begs the question and makes such Christian apologetics more ridiculous in the eyes of sincere men."

Other Reformed Confessions

The Belgic Confession was constructed in 1561. Its author was Guy De Bres who was martyred in 1567. It was written for the churches in Flanders and the Netherlands. The Reformed Synod of Emden adopted it in 1571, and the National Synod of Dort in 1619. It is part of the standards of the Christian Reformed Church in the United States and the Reformed Church in America. Article 4 of the Confession reads as follows:

We receive these books, and these only (i.e., the sixty-six books of the Old and New Testaments) as holy and canonical, for the regulation, foundation, and confirmation of our faith; believing without any doubt all things contained in them, not so much because the Church receives and approves them as such, but more especially because the Holy Ghost witnesseth in our hearts that they are from God, whereof they carry the evidence in themselves. For the very blind are able to perceive that the things foretold in them are fulfilling.

What is taught in the Belgic Confession is what is taught in the Westminster Confession of Faith. These two smaller denominations have been guided by their Belgic Confession and it has occupied a large role in the lives of these two groups. The finest expression of conviction about biblical infallibility was written by Louis Berkhof, a longtime professor at Calvin Seminary. In his *Manual of Doctrine* and *Systematic Theology,* he clearly and forcefully stated the position of the Belgic Confession as the inerrant Word of the living God.

Baptist Confessions

Perhaps no other group of people produced more confessions of faith than the Baptists. This is not wholly surprising, since the Baptists view each local congregation of believers as a true and complete church. Thus no one can ever speak of *the* Baptist Church. There is no such thing. We can only speak of Baptist churches. Any local Baptist congregation can produce its own confession of faith, and many do. No local congregation can bind the conscience of any other local congregation of saints with its confession. Each church is and always has been autonomous in itself. Some Baptist confessions of faith, however, are better than others. In the United States, there have been two major Baptist confessions. And interestingly enough, one of them, the Philadelphia Confession of Faith, owes much to the Westminster Confession of Faith. Its statement on Scripture is the same as that of Westminster. Therefore, to conclude that both teach an infallible Scripture is quite obvious.

The other great United States Baptist confession of faith is the New Hampshire Confession. This Confession was adopted by the messengers to the Southern Baptist Convention annual conclave in 1925. It has been reasserted on several occasions, and is undoubtedly the one statement that comes closest to representing mainstream Southern Baptists who make up the largest non-Catholic religious group in American life. On Scripture, the New Hampshire Confession reads as follows:

We believe that the Holy Bible was written by men divinely inspired, and is a perfect treasure of heavenly instruction: that it has God for its author, salvation for its end, and truth without any mixture of error, for its matter; that it reveals the principles by which God will judge us; and therefore is, and shall remain to the end of the world, the true center of Christian union, and the supreme standard by which all human conduct, creeds, and opinions should be tried.

At a time when so many overemphasize the human aspect of Scripture, it is fair to point out that the New Hampshire Confession proclaims God to be the author of Scripture. It also says there is no mixture of error in Scripture. Some of those who dislike the doctrine of biblical inerrancy have tried to prove that "without any mixture of error" has a limited meaning and does not embrace all of the Bible. It would be impossible to show when this confession was first composed in 1833 that those who wrote the confession had any such reservations in mind. They then believed the Bible to be free from error. Among the Southern Baptists, most of the lay people and large numbers of distinguished scholars through the years have believed that "without any mixture of error" means there are no errors in the Word of God.

The Testimony of Baptist Scholars

One of the great names among the Southern Baptists is that of **James Petigru Boyce**, who occupied the Chair of Systematic Theology at what was then the only Southern Baptist Theological Seminary at Louisville. In his ABSTRACT OF SYSTEMATIC THEOLOGY, Dr. Boyce pointed out one peculiarity about the operation of the Southern Baptist Theological Seminary. He noted that "the subject of inspiration, for special reasons, has been remanded in this special seminary to the department of Biblical Introduction" (p. 35). But he could hardly avoid the subject of inspiration and went on to say about the Bible that:

> No other book has ever been found more reliable whenever its statements could be tested. It carries upon its face everywhere the verisimilitude of truth. Its own testimony is with most persons who read it an all-sufficient evidence of its truthfulness (p. 36).

Dr. Boyce adds this further statement:

> We may argue *a priori* as to the character of this revelation as follows: a. It must come from God...b. It must be suited to our present condition...c. It must be secured from all possibility of error so that its teachings may be relied on with equal, if not greater, confidence than those of reason (p. 37).

The well-known and highly respected **John R. Sampey**, one-time president of the Southern Baptist Theological Seminary at Louisville and professor of Old Testament Interpretation, believed in an inerrant Bible. In his *Syllabus for Old Testament Study,* copyrighted in 1903, Dr. Sampey spoke of the difference between the radical and the conservative views of the Bible. He went on record as a Conservative and said, "Conservatives hold that the writers were preserved from all error by the inbreathed Spirit guiding them. Radicals reject such a theory with scorn. Some Liberals believe in a sort of inspiration which heightened the spiritual perceptions of the scriptural writers, but did not preserve them from error." He went on to say that Conservatives believe that what Jesus says puts an end to further argument, "whereas Radicals set aside His authority entirely, and Moderate Liberals point to the limitations of His knowledge as a man. Jesus has Himself said that the Scriptures cannot be broken (John 10:35). If Radical critics break the Scriptures, they will also break the authority of Jesus as our Divine *Teacher*" (pp. 59,60).

B.H. Carroll was a famed Southern Baptist teacher at Baylor who founded Southwestern Baptist Theological Seminary, now located in Fort Worth, Texas. Dr. Carroll started a seminary that is now the largest theological seminary in the world with more than three thousand students. He was a gifted linguist, a sterling scholar, and a popular author. In his book, *Inspiration of the Bible* (New York: Revell, 1930), Dr. Carroll states his own belief in plenary, verbal inspiration of the original Scriptures. He indicates that, at best, there are only a smattering of unresolved textual questions. He answers the objections of critics in penetrating fashion. A few excerpts from his book will show how strong his commitment was to an inerrant Scripture:

It has always been a matter of profound surprise to me that anybody should ever question the verbal inspiration of the Bible.

The whole thing had to be written in words. Words are signs of ideas, and if the words are not inspired, then there is no way of getting at anything in connection with inspiration. If I am free to pick up the Bible and read something and say, 'That is inspired,' then read something else and say, 'That is not inspired,' and someone else does not agree with me as to which is and which is not inspired, it leaves the whole thing unsettled as to whether any of it is inspired.

What is the object of inspiration? It is to put accurately, in human words, ideas from God. If the words are not inspired, how am I to know how much to reject, and how to find out whether anything is from God? When you hear the silly talk that the Bible 'contains' the word of God and is not the word of God, you hear a fool's talk. I don't care if he is a Doctor of Divinity, a President of a University covered with medals from universities of Europe and the United States, it is fool-talk.

There can be no inspiration of the book without the inspiration of the words of the book (p. 20).

The Holy Spirit guided the men in the selection of material, even where that material came from some other book, even an uninspired book, the Spirit guiding in selecting and omitting material (p. 22).

There were no shorthand reporters in those days, and there is not a man on earth who could, after a lapse of fifty years, recall *verbatim et literatim* what Christ said, and yet John, without a shadow of hesitancy, goes on and gives page after page of what Christ said just after the institution of the Lord's Supper. Inspiration in that case was exercised in awakening the memory so that John could reproduce these great orations of Christ.

Of the orations of Paul, take that speech recorded in Acts 13, an exceedingly remarkable speech, or the one recorded in Acts 26, or the one on Mars' Hill, in chapter 17, one of the most finished productions that the world has ever seen. Inspiration enabled Luke to report exactly what Paul said. Luke never could have done that unassisted. Luke, as a man, might have given the substance, but that is not the substance, it is an elaborate report, the sense depending upon the words used (p. 23).

Now we come to an important point. When these inspired declarations were written, they were absolutely infallible. Take these Scriptures: John 10:35, "The scripture cannot be broken"; Matthew 5:18, "Till heaven and earth shall pass away, one jot or tittle shall in no wise pass away from the law, till all things be accomplished"; Acts 1:16, "It was needful that the scripture should be fulfilled."

That is one of the most important points in connection with inspiration, viz: that the inspired word is irrefragable, infallible; that all the powers of the world cannot break one "thus saith the Lord" (p. 25).

Charles Haddon Spurgeon represents Baptists in Britain in the late nineteenth century. He was surely one of the greatest pulpiteers among Baptists in the last century. He was a great evangelist, and it may be said without fear of contradiction that there has never been a great soul winner who did not believe the Bible to be the infallible Word of God. Mr. Spurgeon, in 1855, preached a sermon, a part of which was devoted to biblical infallibility. He said:

Then, since God wrote it, mark its truthfulness. If I had written it, there would be worms of critics who would at once swarm on it, and would cover it with their evil spawn; had I written it, there would be men who would pull it to pieces at once, and perhaps quite right too. But this is the Word of God. Come, search, ye critics, and find an error. This is a vein of pure gold, unalloyed by quartz or any earthly substance. This is a star without a speck; a sun without a blot; a light without darkness; a moon without paleness; a glory without a dimness. O Bible! it cannot be said of any other book, that it is perfect and pure; but of thee we can declare all wisdom is gathered up in thee, without a particle of folly. This is the judge that ends the strife where wit and reason fail. This is the book untainted by any error, but is pure, unalloyed, perfect truth. Why? Because God wrote it. Ah! charge God with error if you please; tell Him that His book is not what it ought to be...Blessed Bible, thou art all truth (Russell H. Conwell, *The Life of Charles Haddon Spurgeon* [Edgewood Publishing Company, 1892), pp. 574-6).

Alvah Hovey, president of Newton Theological Institute (which was later joined with Andover to become Andover Newton), defended biblical inerrancy. He argued against those who said that "infallibility in the original Scriptures requires for its complement infallibility in all copies, translations, and, some would say, interpretations of them. For otherwise, we are told, the benefit of infallibility is lost to all but the primitive readers. But this, again, is a mistake; for the errors from transcription, translations, etc., are such as can be detected, or at least estimated, and reduced to a minimum; while errors in the original revelation could not be measured" (*Manual of Systematic Theology and Christian Ethics* [Philadelphia: A.B.P.S., 1880], p. 83). Hovey was saying clearly that biblical inerrancy was the common viewpoint, but it was being challenged. And he responded to those who offered that challenge. He pursued this theme by alluding to questions of historical and scientific errors.

Hovey said, "On the supposed historical errors of the Bible we remark, (1) They relate, for the most part, to matters of chronology, generally numbers, etc. (2) Transcribers are specially liable to mistakes in copying numbers, names, etc. (3) Different names for the same person, and different termini for the same period are quite frequent. (4) Round numbers are often employed for specific. Making proper allowance for these facts we deny that historical errors are found in the Bible." He also dealt with the so-called scientific errors, saying, "All references to matters of science in the Bible are (1) Merely incidental and auxiliary; (2) Clothed in popular language; and (3) Confirmed by consciousness, so far as they relate to the mind. Remembering these facts, we say that the Bible has not been shown to contain scientific errors--astronomy, geology, ethnology...Bearing in mind these facts, it will be impossible for us to find in the Bible any contradictions which mar its excellence" (*Ibid.*, p. 85).

Lutheran Confessions

In the United States, Lutheranism is represented by a number of different groups who have adopted confessions of faith in which they speak about their attachment to the Bible as the Word of God. Only one of the major Lutheran groups of which I have knowledge does not have a statement of Scripture that commits the denomination to inerrancy. This is the Lutheran Church in America, a recent emergent which is theologically the most liberal of the Lutheran groups. The others, as we shall now see, made formal commitments to inerrancy.

The American Lutheran Church

The American Lutheran Church is headquartered in Minneapolis. In 1925 the "Minneapolis Theses," the first basic theological document for this denomination, contained a statement about the Bible. The document accepted the canonical Scriptures "as a whole and in all their parts as the divinely inspired, revealed, and inerrant Word of God." In 1956 when the proposed constitution for the new American Lutheran Church was voted on by the Evangelical Lutheran Church, the same statement about the canonical Scriptures was written into it.

The Lutheran Church--Missouri Synod

The Missouri Synod Lutherans are generally of German background. From its inception, this church committed itself to an inerrant Scripture. Like most of the Lutheran churches, it held in highest esteem the Augsburg Confession as well as the Smalcald Articles, the two Catechisms of Luther, and the Formula of Concord. Lutherans were generally agreed that Luther himself held to an inerrant Scripture as has already been stated. But when doubt began to creep in, the Missouri Synod took steps to spell out more specifically under modern conditions the more exact nature of the denomination's commitment to a trustworthy Bible.

In 1932 the Missouri Synod adopted a *Brief Statement* of its doctrinal position. In 1947, at the centennial celebration of the denomination, the *Brief Statement* was incorporated in the official proceedings of the convention (Proceedings, 1932, p. 1548), although it was not made part of the Constitution. The first article of the *Brief Statement* said this about Scripture:

1. We teach that the Holy Scriptures differ from all other books in the world in that they are the Word of God. They are the Word of God because the holy men of God who wrote the Scriptures wrote only that which the Holy Ghost communicated to them by inspiration, 2 Tim. 3:16; 2 Pet. 1:21. We teach also that the verbal inspiration of the Scriptures is not a so-called "theological deduction," but that it is taught by direct statements of the Scriptures, 2 Tim. 3:16, John 10:35; Rom. 3:2; 1 Cor. 2:13. Since the Holy Scriptures are the Word of God, it goes without saying that they contain no errors or contradictions, but that they are in all their parts and words the infallible truth, also in those parts which treat of historical, geographical, and other secular matters, John 10:35.

The Missouri Synod has experienced some severe problems concerning the inerrancy of Scripture and it has repeated its commitment to the *Brief Statement* several times since 1947. At the moment the denomination is solidly and fervently committed to this view of the Bible.

The Wisconsin Evangelical Lutheran Synod

The Wisconsin Evangelical Lutheran Synod is the last Lutheran denomination we will mention. It is also committed to an inerrant Scripture and has spelled it out very specifically in published form in a pamphlet titled *This We Believe*. Among the statements in this pamphlet the following are representative of Wisconsin's commitment:

We believe that in a miraculous way that goes beyond all human investigation God the Holy Ghost inspired these men to write His Word. These "holy men of God spoke as they were moved by the Holy Ghost" (II Pet. 1:21). What they said, was spoken "not in the words which man's wisdom teacheth, but which the Holy Ghost teacheth" (I Cor. 2:13). Every thought they expressed, every word they used, was given them by the Holy Spirit by inspiration. St. Paul wrote to Timothy: "All scripture is given by inspiration of God" (II Tim. 3:16). We therefore believe in the verbal inspiration of the Scriptures, not a mechanical dictation, but a word-for-word inspiration...

We believe that Scripture is a unified whole, true and without error in everything it says; for our Savior said "The scripture cannot be broken" (John 10:35)...

We reject any thought that makes only part of Scripture God's Word, that allows for the possibility of factual error in Scripture, also in so-called nonreligious matters (for example, historical, geographical).

We reject all views that fail to acknowledge the Holy Scriptures as God's revelation and Word. We likewise reject all views that see in them merely a human record of God's revelation as he encounters man in history apart from the Scriptures, and so a record subject to human imperfections.

At the conclusion of the Statement about the Bible, these words appear, "This is what Scripture teaches about God and His Revelation. This we believe, teach and confess."

Whatever may be the situation with respect to individuals within any of these denominations today, we can say with emphasis that each formally adopted a statement that is in line with the historic commitment of the Church of Jesus Christ through the ages. And these statements bear witness to the fact that disbelief in inerrancy is a modern, not an ancient, phenomenon.

The Anglicans and Methodists

What has been said of the Reformers and of the Baptists may also be said about the Anglicans and the Methodists. But they came out of a different tradition, and their views must be understood within that context. The Anglican Church came into being as a direct result of Henry the VIII's marriage dilemma with Catholic Catherine whom he wished to divorce. When the papacy refused to accede to his desires, Henry broke with the pope and established his own church. But that church stood then, and remains, in the tradition of Catholicism. It traces its apostolic succession back to the apostles and believes as Roman Catholics do in the historical episcopate. It accepts the real presence of Christ in the sacrament of the supper, and in a number of ways stands within the tradition of Roman Catholicism. Among the doctrines it inherited from the Roman Church was its view of the Bible as the infallible Word of God. It rejected some of Rome's teaching, such as those of the seven sacraments, the headship of the pope, and the like. But it did not declare itself against the Roman Catholic Church's teaching with respect to biblical infallibility. It followed this doctrinal teaching until it, like so many of the denominations that sprang out of the Reformation period, discarded it in the late nineteenth and twentieth centuries. (There are still some orthodox Anglicans who stand in the tradition of evangelical Christianity and still believe in an infallible Bible.)

The Methodist denomination came from the loins of Anglicanism and its founder, John Wesley, lived and died within the fold of the Anglican faith. Like the Anglican Church, Methodism believed in an infallible Scripture. Neither the Anglicans nor the Methodists enshrined their belief in an infallible Scripture in creeds and confessions with the precision and accuracy that marked those of the Reformed tradition, the Baptists, and the Lutherans. This may also explain why it was that the Anglicans and the Methodists were the most easily led astray from a commitment to biblical infallibility, and why these two groups in our generation include among their numbers large bodies of theological liberals whose beliefs are quite extreme.

George A. Turner of the evangelical Asbury Theological Seminary wrote this about John Wesley:

Wesley believed in the full inspiration and inerrancy of the Bible. His view would now be described as pre-critical, as would the view of most eighteenth-century writers. The problem of authority which Luther faced was less acute in Wesley's day than the problem of indifference in the Church. Thus Wesley was less bold than Luther in determining the relative value of different books of the Bible; to him they were all equally inspired and hence authoritative...he did not feel the need of establishing the authority of the Bible or defending it from destructive critics. Jean Astruc, "the father of Pentateuchal criticism," published his views on the authorship of Genesis in 1753, but there is no evidence that it was noticed by Wesley and his colleagues (George A. Turner, "John Wesley as an Interpreter of Scripture," in *Inspiration and Interpretation,* John W. Walvoord, ed. [Grand Rapids: Eerdmans, 1957], p. 161).

Wesley's own view of the Bible was a high one indeed. He never believed for a moment that because the writers of Scripture were human they therefore erred in what they wrote. In his *Journal* he wrote, "Nay, if there be any mistakes in the Bible there may as well be a thousand. If there be one falsehood in that book it did not come from the God of truth" (John Wesley, *Journal*, VI, 117). It would be inaccurate to suggest that Wesley spent much time on the question of biblical infallibility. He believed it and so did those who became Methodists. He preached, taught, and labored on the basis of his underlying conviction that the Bible is the inerrant Word of God.

Among the Anglicans and the Methodists today there are strong defenders of biblical inerrancy just as there are strong opponents of that viewpoint. And no one can suppose for a moment that either of these denominations now or in the discernible future will become strong advocates of inerrancy.

Concluding Observations

The facts that we have just mentioned are by no means all that can be said about Christians who believed the Bible to be inerrant. Scores and scores of scholars in the 19th century professed and wrote about their belief in an inerrant Scripture. The Editor of the *Prairie Overcomer,* T.S. Rendall, wrote a long article titled *Anatomy of a Ghost* in the September 1976 issue of that magazine. In it he quoted Professor Charles A. Briggs who made the remark, "The theory that the Bible is inerrant is the ghost of modern evangelicalism to frighten children." Mr. Rendall went on from there to show that any number of excellent scholars in North America, Britain, and the Continent of Europe in the 19th century held to the highest possible view of the Bible and its complete trustworthiness. The list and the quotations are impressive and they are accurate.

In the same issue of this magazine, the editor reprinted a short article written by Thomas Witherow who was a professor of church history at Magee College, Londonderry, in 1865. The thrust of the article showed that all of Scripture is profitable not just parts of it. This beautifully written and adequate defense of the inerrancy of all of Scripture is quoted herewith (*The Apostolic Church,* pp. 91 ff.).

All Scripture Is Profitable

It is very common for professing Christians to draw a distinction between *essentials* and *non-essentials* in religion, and to infer that, if any fact or doctrine rightly belongs to the latter class, it must be a matter of very little importance, and may in practice be safely set at nought.

The great bulk of men take their opinions on trust; they will not undergo the toil of thinking, searching, and reasoning about anything. And one of the most usual expedients adopted to save them the trouble of inquiry, and to turn aside the force of any disagreeable fact, is to meet it by saying, "The matter is not essential to salvation; therefore we need give ourselves little concern on the subject."

Dangerous Distinction

If the distinction here specified is safe, the inference drawn from it is certainly dangerous. To say that, because a fact of divine revelation is not essential to salvation, it must of necessity be unimportant, and may or may not be received by us, is to assert a principle, the application of which would make havoc of our Christianity.

For, what are the truths essential to salvation? Are they not these: that there is a God; that all men are sinners; that the Son of God died upon the cross to make atonement for the guilty; and that whosoever believes on the Lord Jesus Christ shall be saved? There is good reason for believing that not a few souls are now in happiness, who in life knew little more than these--the first principles of the oracles of God--the very alphabet of the Christian system; and if so, no other divine truths can be counted absolutely essential to salvation.

But if all the other truths of revelation are unimportant, because they happen to be non-essentials, it follows that the Word of God itself is in the main unimportant; for by far the greatest portion of it is occupied with matters, the knowledge of which, in the case supposed, is not absolutely indispensable to the everlasting happiness of men.

Nor does it alter the case, if we regard the number of fundamental truths to be much greater. Let a man once persuade himself that importance attaches only to what he is pleased to call essentials, whatever their number, and he will, no doubt, shorten his creed and cut away the foundation of many controversies; but he will practically set aside all except a very small part of the Scriptures. If such a principle does not mutilate the Bible, it stigmatises much of it as trivial. Revelation is all gold for preciousness and purity, but the very touch of such a principle would transmute the most of it into dross.

Every Statement Important

Though every statement in the Scripture cannot be regarded as absolutely essential to salvation, yet everything there is essential to some other wise and important end, else it would not find a place in the good Word of God. Human wisdom may be baffled in attempting to specify the design of every truth that forms a component part of divine revelation, but eternity will show us that no portion of it is useless.

All Scripture is profitable. A fact written therein may not be essential to human salvation, and yet it may be highly conducive to some other great and gracious purpose in the economy of God--it may be necessary for our personal comfort, for our guidance in life, or for our growth in holiness, and most certainly it is essential to the completeness of the system of divine truth. The law of the Lord is perfect.

Strike out of the Bible the truth that seems the most insignificant of all, and the law of the Lord would not be perfect any more. In architecture, the pinning that fills a crevice in the wall occupies a subordinate position, in comparision with the quoin; but the builder lets us know that the one has an important purpose to serve as well as the other, and does its part to promote the stability and completeness of the house.

In shipbuilding, the screws and bolts that gird the ship together are insignificant, as compared with the beams of oak and masts of pine, but they contribute their full share to the safety of the vessel and the security of the passenger. So in the Christian system, every fact, great or small, that God has been pleased to insert in the Bible is, by its very position, invested with importance, answers its end, and, though justly considered as non-essential to salvation, does not deserve to be accounted as worthless.

Every divine truth is important, though it may be that all divine truths are not of equal importance. The simplest statement of the Bible is of more concern to an immortal being than the most sublime sentiment of mere human genius. The one carries with it what the other cannot show--the stamp of the approval of God. The one comes to us from Heaven, the other savours of the earth. The one has for us a special interest, as forming a constituent portion of that Word which is a message from God to each individual man; the other is the production of a mind merely human, to which we and all our interests were alike unknown.

A Light to our Feet

Any truth merely human should weigh with us light as a feather in comparison with the most insignificant of the truths of God. The faith of a Christian should strive to reach and grasp everything that God has honoured with a place in that Word, the design of which is to be a light to our feet as we thread our way through this dark world. Besides, this, unlike every other book, is not doomed to perish. Heaven and earth may pass away, but the words of Christ shall not pass away. The seal of eternity is stamped on every verse of the Bible. This fact is enough of itself to make every line of it important.

As we end this part of our journey together, we may conclude: 1) The doctrine of biblical inerrancy has a history as long as the history of the Christian Church and existed before the New Testament was written; 2) The Church before, during, and after the Reformation witnessed to the inerrancy of the Bible in its totality, and numberless scholars attested to its integrity and truthfulness; 3) It was not until the eighteenth century that men began to question the truthfulness of Scripture in any number and began to attack it as containing error; 4) These attacks on Scripture derive from a common stream of scholastic presuppositions, the acceptance of which can only lead to a denial of the inerrancy of the Bible.

It is most important that those who believe the Bible should know what the cause for destroying the Bible is, and be able to respond to those who make use of this methodology, of which we shall be speaking shortly. Suffice it to say at this moment that the best of those who use the methodology we will examine must seek to find the Word of God in Scripture. And for the worst of them, the Scriptures are not thought to be the Word of God at all. So we take a look at the historical-critical method which lies at the bottom of the denial of the inerrancy of Scripture.

The Historical-Critical Method, the Bible's Greatest Opponent

The Bible has a number of enemies. Chief among them, and the father of all efforts to destroy the written Word of God, is Satan. He uses atheists, agnostics, secularists, quasi-Christians, and even genuine believers to accomplish his malign purposes.

Satan

Satan not only hates God who is the author of Scripture; he also hates the Word that God has authored. The reason is simple enough. God is truth. Satan is a liar and the father of lies. He will stoop to anything, but we must not think of him as a horned demon with a pitchfork in his hand. Nor must we suppose he doesn't know the Word of God. He knows it from cover to cover. In the temptation of Jesus, he unconsciously bears witness to its truth and its universal application. "It is written," he said, but what good is this if it isn't true, if it can't be trusted, or if it doesn't have application for all ages? Satan knows and proclaims the Word of God to be true even though he rejects it.

Satan is the highest created being in the order of the angelic host. He is brilliant, clever, scheming, and malicious. He is a master of the soft sell, a genius at misrepresentation, a subtle rascal who, if we saw him walking down Broadway in New York City, would appear so attractive, so debonair, so harmless, that we would look at him twice. We'd like to know a chap like this, and if he appeared on the stage as a star, we would give him a standing ovation. Indeed he *is* an actor whose stage face we see, whose real self is hidden from sight.

But Satan has limitations. Thank God he can only be in one place at one time. But he has helpers who do his bidding. The fallen angels are a part of his army. So is every unbeliever, and so may be some born-again Christians who have fallen into his clutches. He uses every human being he can to hurt the Lord Jesus and defeat His cause.

The chief point of Satan's attack is to bring God before the dock and make Him out to be a liar. It really isn't strange that the greatest liar of all should represent God the creator as a liar to men. Satan's dart is intended to convince men that God either never said what God claimed He said, or that what He did say is to be questioned and doubted.

Adam and Eve

The fall of Adam and Eve constitutes a paradigm of Satan's method of operating. He has not varied the pattern to this very hour. Satan, who appeared to Eve in the form of the serpent, engaged her in an innocuous conversation that was simple enough. He asked her a leading question, a question that was designed to raise doubt in Eve's mind. "Yea, hath God said, 'Ye shall not eat of every tree of the garden?' " (Genesis 3:1).

First, we perceive that he knew that God had told Adam and Even what they could and they could not do. His first words show his wickedness and manifest his malignant spirit.

Eve's reply was this, in effect, "No, you do not really know what God said. He said we can eat the fruit of the trees in the Garden, except for the fruit of the tree which is in the midst of the Garden." Eve knew she could eat of the tree of life which was in the garden, but Satan craftily made no reference to the tree of life.

Eve did something else. She added to the words of God's command. She said that God said of the tree of the knowledge of good and evil, "Neither shall ye touch it." Now evidently God did not forbid them to touch the fruit of that tree. But may not Eve have grasped a truth we overlook? If she did not handle the fruit, she could not eat it. Did she not somehow realize that even to handle it would lead to eating it, and that in turn would lead to death?

Nobody commits adultery out of the blue. There are always preparatory steps that precede the fatal step. David would never have committed adultery with Bathsheba, if he had not seen her bathing on the rooftop. It was the sight of **Bathsheba** that inflamed his appetite. But it could have ended there. Instead, he sent for her. And it could have ended there, if she had refused to come. She was no less guilty than he. But before they were locked in their sinful embrace, there were decisions they made before the fact that led at last to the tragedy. So also with Eve in relation to Satan's fiery dart.

Satan's answer to Eve was sly. He intimated that what God said was either designed to scare them or that even if it were real, it would hardly come to pass, "You shall not surely die." "Ah, no," Satan said, "if you eat, the result will surprise and thrill you. Ye shall be as gods, knowing good and evil." So she ate and gave to Adam to eat and they died--because they chose to disbelieve the Word of the living God.

There is one weapon that Satan uses today, an effective weapon which has brought manifold hurt to the Church of Jesus Christ and has wrought untold damage in the lives of multitudes. It has produced numerous heresies, quenched the fires of evangelism, and extinguished the passion for world missionary outreach in many places. It is an enemy of the Bible which it persistently undermines, and which it claims to be defective and, at least in parts, untrue. I am talking about:

The Historical-Critical Method

It is a big claim to assert that the use of *the* historical-critical method is a chief cause that makes necessary a book like this which proclaims that the Bible is the inerrant Word of God. But this is the fact. Where did the historical-critical method come from, what does it stand for, how is it being used, and why is it baneful?

Where It Came From

The historical-critical method is a relatively recent phenomenon in the long history of the Church. It goes back two centuries to Europe, and is most closely associated with the name of Johann Salomo Semler who is regarded as its originator. Professor Semler taught at the University of Halle.

This university was steeped and grounded in pietism, which was a response to German theological rationalism that emphasized head knowledge without an accompanying heart response. In its early days, Halle produced an incomparable company of missionary volunteers who went to the ends of the earth with the Gospel. It was inappropriate and unexpected that a University of this sort should later become the fountainhead of a methodology that would seek to destroy the written Word of God. But it did. In the case of J.S. Semler we have a son of a German Lutheran pietist minister who rejected his father's pietism. The pendulum swung full scale in the opposite direction. What was there about the views of this professor that hurt Scripture?

What Its Presuppositions Are

Professor Eugene F. Klug, a Lutheran scholar, in a foreword to Gerhard Maier's book, *The End of the Historical Critical Method*, pinpoints the problem. He says that Semler

> *not only handled the Bible as an object for historical scrutiny and criticism, but also as a book little different from and no more holy than any other, and surely not to be equated with the Word of God.* Very plainly he was saying that he rejected the divine inspiration of the text. This was but a symptom of his total theological stance, a tip of the iceberg so to speak. His was really a revolt against miracles and the supernatural in general, and against heaven in particular. God's supernatural activity in history simply was not in Semler's "book." Not unexpectedly, under his and others' hand, the Bible text and content suffered deliberate vivisection. The surgery was often quite radical and overt, without benefit of anaesthesia for those directly affected by it in the churches (p. 8).

Gerhard Maier finds in one sentence from a book by Professor Semler the fundamental thesis of the historical-critical method. Semler said, "The root of the evil (in theology) is the interchangeable use of the terms 'Scripture' and 'Word of God' " (*Ibid.,* p. 15). What does this mean?

Dr. Semler and those who follow this method today are saying Scripture is not *the* Word of God. There is the Word of God which may be found *in* Scripture, but much of Scripture cannot be called the Word of God.

Let's say it another way. The Church has always recognized that the canonical books constitute the Word of God. Once a New Testament book is regarded as canonical it is *the* Word of God. But when anyone says that Scripture and the Word of God are not synonymous, we have the problem of discovering what part of the canon is the Word of God. This makes it essential to find "the canon in the canon." So, says Maier, a modern German scholar, E. Kaesemann (*Das Neue Testament als Kanon,* Goettingen, 1970), can say that "in the New Testament, faith and superstition are both in the arena at the same time; he therefore wants to retreat from the incomprehensible...'superstition that everywhere in the canon only genuine faith is proclaimed' " (*Ibid.,* p. 15).

A word is in order about the meaning of the terms "historical" and "critical." What Semler, modern scholars, and historians mean by the use of the word "historical" is that the Bible is like any other book and can be approached the same way we approach any other book. When this is done, it effectively destroys the Bible.

Approaching the Bible historically as we approach any other book is wrong in principle for several reasons. First, the Bible is the only book that has God for its author. Thus, it is unique. Second, the historical approach engenders doubt and produces disbelief. In the historical approach, the user can state his doubts particularly with respect to things that happened only once and for which there is no historical evidence. But if we come to the Scripture from the theological-biblical standpoint, we can assume that anything the Bible states to have happened is possible.

No historical approach can verify the one-time virgin birth, or the incarnation, or the meaning of Christ's death on Calvary.

The use of the word "critical" is far more serious than that of the word "historical." We can and should have a properly defined "historical-biblical method" rather than a "critical" one. Indeed, the word "critical" includes the presupposition that not all of the Bible is the Word of God. The critical method works to find the canon in the canon, but it is impossible to do this. And no two modern critics have ever come up with the same answers.

The "critical" approach starts with the assumption that the Bible is composed of a divine Scripture and a human Scripture. But the Bible does not allow for itself to be so divided. It ends in subjectivity; for each man must discover the Word of God for himself, and why should someone else's conclusions bind my conscience?

Gerhard Maier correctly observes, "The higher-critical method, as a matter of basic principle, means a procedure in which the Bible is approached from an extra-Biblical position and with extra-Biblical standards, with the objective of discovering the Word of God in the process" (op. cit., p. 24).

At the heart of the higher-critical method lies the assumption that there is something that stands above Scripture, that can pass judgment on Scripture; and whatever that is, it is superior to the Bible as the source of religious knowledge. This cannot be.

How the Higher Critical Method Is Used

What we have said so far is but the briefest account of a complex and difficult matter that most people do not know about, or fail to understand. It should not be passed over lightly, however, and Christians should make a serious effort to understand it, for the use of the higher-critical or historical-critical method lies at the heart of persistent attacks waged against an infallible Scripture.

For a moment, consideration must be given to the way in which the principles of the historical-critical method are consciously or unconsciously applied (sometimes by earnest Christians); and in the process they effectively destroy scriptural infallibility and force people to find "the canon in the canon."

Revelational and Non-Revelational Scripture

Some say there are two kinds of Scripture, revelational and non-revelational. Revelational Scripture is absolutely trustworthy; non-revelational Scripture has error in it. The true Word of God is found in revelational Scripture.

As soon as this distinction is made, trouble begins. The distinction does not come from the Bible itself. It comes from the outside, and is imposed on Scripture. This principle destroys the objective status of the Bible and throws it into the realm of the subjective immediately. It also connotes the mistaken notion that Scripture is composed of that which is human and fallible as well as that which is divine and infallible.

Who decides what Scripture is revelational and true, over against that which is non-revelational and erroneous? Each reader of the Bible must decide this for himself, and there is no single standard against which the opinions of men can be weighed. What I think, will differ from what you think, and no two people think alike. Those who hold this view must search for the canon in the canon. And they will never find it. They are lost on the sea of subjectivity.

Science versus Scripture

Can the Bible be trusted in matters of history and the cosmos? Francis Schaeffer has asked this question and written a small book to defend the truthfulness of the first eleven chapters of Genesis, which speak of creation and of the first man, Adam.

At stake here are several issues. One is whether the account of Adam's creation can be harmonized with the prevailing views of so many scientists, including some Christian scientists who are evolutionists. The second issue is whether the Bible is telling us the truth when it says Adam was the first man, and that Cain and Abel were his sons.

One thing stands out starkly. The Bible itself says that Adam was an immediate creation and he was the first man. The genealogical tables in Chronicles and in Luke pinpoint the fact that these writers believed and taught that the whole of the human race has descended from Adam.

In the book of Romans, Paul speaks of the first and second Adam. He also teaches that sin entered the human race through Adam. If there was no first Adam, then sin could not have entered through a non-existent person. If the first Adam was not a person, why should we believe the second Adam was historical?

If Adam really was the first man, but came in evolutionary fashion from a sub-human form of life, then the biblical account must be myth or saga. But if it is not historical, why should we believe that part of it which says Adam was the first man?

Whichever way men explain away the straightforward account of Scripture about the creation of Adam and the fact that he was the first man, they end up by introducing into Scripture one of the principles that is intrinsic to the liberal historical-critical method. They are saying the Bible is not telling us the truth, and they are putting the views of Science above Scripture—to sit in judgment on Scripture. However, once this is done, the end is the same. Not all of Scripture is the Word of God, and you must find the canon in the canon. Subjectivity reigns and the objective character of revelation is lost.

Faith and Practice

We have noted that some limit biblical authority and trustworthiness to matters of faith and practice. This means that Scripture has error in it, in matters that do not pertain to faith and practice. But nowhere in Scripture is any distinction made by which it can be determined what parts of Scripture do not pertain to matters of faith and practice.

Once Scripture is breached and error acknowledged, holding to infallibility in matters of faith and practice loses credibility. Immediately, we must determine what the specific matters of faith are. Is the virgin birth a matter of faith? There are many who say that the virgin birth of Jesus is an explanation to account for the incarnation, but it never really happened. Jesus, they say, actually had a human father. Once you open the door to error, it is impossible to deliver matters of faith and practice from ambiguity, compromise, and denial.

A seminary professor a few years ago polled the faculties of a number of institutions. He found out that 40% of the professors did not believe that Jesus is God. They are unitarians. If Scripture has error in it, who is to say with any assurance that the deity of Jesus is true? If there are historical errors, may not His deity be one of them?

In that event it cannot be a matter of faith, for it wouldn't be true. And what is not true, plainly ought not to be asserted or believed.

Once you say that the truthfulness of Scripture is limited to matters of faith and practice, you have fallen into one of the presuppositions of higher criticism which teaches that not all of Scripture is the Word of God. You are right back trying to find the canon in the canon, with the loss of objectivity and submissions to subjectivity in place thereof.

Ethics

In the area of ethics, the key question revolves around matters of practice, i.e., how I live and conduct myself--the day by day decisions of life. We will assume for a moment in this connection that the infallibility of the Bible is limited to matters of faith *and* practice. But we will see that the same old problems arise and even those Scriptures that are supposed to be true are not really true.

We have already quoted a former theological seminary dean who, among other things, said that "bad ethical standards" are found in the Bible. Certainly this involves matters of practice and, believe it or not, matters of faith. We will introduce a second illustration before drawing a conclusion.

A recent writer discusses the teaching of the Bible about the relationship of husband and wife. This is part and parcel of the Christian ethic and a matter of practice. In his discussion, the writer says that the apostle Paul taught subordination of the wife to the husband in the book of Ephesians. Then he says that what Paul taught in Galatians contradicts what he taught in Ephesians. He concludes that the teaching in Ephesians is rabbinical teaching that may have been true at one time, but certainly is no longer because of the new teaching in Galatians. What do we say to all of this?

Both cases illustrate the same point. Some of the ethical teachings having to do with matters of practice are not true. They are erroneous. Whatever is erroneous cannot be the Word of God, for God cannot teach error or tell us to do what is wrong. Let's be very specific. If Paul's teaching in Ephesians is wrong, then there is wrong ethical teaching and at least this part of Ephesians cannot be the Word of God.

If Paul is in error in one of his ethical teachings, how do I know he is right in any other teachings? Which teachings shall I accept or reject, and why? Curiously, the book of Galatians was written *before* the book of Ephesians. Since Ephesians came later, should we not suppose that the later teaching is the correct one? Why should I accept Galatians over Ephesians, or vice versa? Surely Galatians and Ephesians are not in conflict with each other. Galatians says that there is neither male nor female in Christ. But this refers to the believer's relationship to Christ in salvation and has nothing whatever to do with the headship of the husband in marriage.

Since the writer of whom we speak here professes to believe the Bible to be the infallible rule of faith *and* practice, we quickly perceive that he has consciously or unconsciously fallen into the subjective mode of life and of necessity must find the canon in the canon. In other words, he must find the canon in the canon even in matters of faith and practice, as well as in matters that are not supposed to relate to faith and practice. The human words of the Bible and the divine words must be found and separated. And even if this were right in principle—which it isn't—no one has been able to do this, for it cannot be done.

Situationism

If in ethics the question we have just discussed is ruinous of Scripture, situation ethics goes far beyond this and involves a principle of biblical interpretation that coincides with the presuppositions of higher criticism.

At least in the discussion of ethics, the presumption is that while there are bad ethics in the Bible there are good ethics as well. And this approach supposes that there are some good ethics, which are absolute and ought not to be broken.

Situation ethics relativizes all of ethics except perhaps for an ill-defined or undefined law of love. This viewpoint says that no one needs to make a decision on the basis of any human or divine rules or laws that are always true and always binding. The circumstances, not any rules, determine what the decision should be.

Situation ethics says that it is impossible to say that lying, cheating, stealing, fornication, adultery, homosexuality, drunkenness, murder, or anything else is absolute. It may be right and proper to do any one of these things depending on the circumstances, and no one can say in advance what is right; and it can only be known by the person who makes the immediate existential decision in his situation.

Now it is true that there are many things about which the Bible says nothing. It certainly does not say whether men should or should not have beards, whether women should wear lipstick and paint their fingernails. But where the Bible does speak and where it lays down absolutes such as in the commandments of God, it can never be right to do for any reason what they specifically prohibit.

Situation ethics destroys the normativity of Scripture in matters of practice, and when this is done a principle inherent in the historical-critical method takes precedence over the principle of Scripture. The search then is on to find the canon, for all of Scripture is no longer the Word of God. Subjectivity once again reigns supreme, and the objectivity of the Bible is lost.

Hermeneutics

The use of wrong principles of hermeneutics (interpretation) introduces into Scripture that which once again forces the reader to search for the canon in the canon. A few illustrations will suffice.

There are biblical scholars who say that Paul did not write the book of Ephesians or the Pastoral Epistles and that Peter did not write 2 Peter. In all of these cases, the books in question claim to have been written by Paul or Peter, as the case may be.

There are Bible scholars who say that the Book of Jonah is fiction, not fact, although the words of Jesus show that He considered it to be factual and not fictional. Other scholars say that Isaiah 40-66 was not written by the prophet Isaiah, although John's Gospel asserts that the second half of the book is Isaianic. Some scholars claim that the book of Daniel was written after the events (around 167 B.C.), instead of before the events prophesied (around 600 B.C.) which the book itself makes clear.

Years ago, Bishop G. Bromley Oxnam of the Methodist Church said that God never ordered the slaughter of the Midianites and any God who did this is a "Dirty Bully." Yet the Scripture says God did just that, and claims that God is holy, just, and righteous.

Still others say that God did not and could not have ordered Abraham to offer up Isaac as a burnt offering on Mt. Moriah. What does all of this mean?

In every case, it means that people who hold these views reject what the Scriptures assert. They do it, not on the basis of Scripture, but on the basis of so-called evidence outside of Scripture that is used to judge Scripture. Or they do it because it is their subjective opinion that what happened is not credible. Now if what these critics assert is true, then at least these parts of the Bible are untrue. And what is untrue cannot be the Word of God.

We are right back in the same muddle. We must find the canon in the canon, and this cannot be done. Moreover if that which claims to have been written by Paul, for example, was not written by Paul, why should we believe the rest of it, when we can't believe what it claims about the authorship?

When the interpretation of Scripture negates Scripture, then Scripture's uniqueness has been fractured, its infallibility sundered, and once more subjectivity is the order of the day.

Redaction Criticism

Two other illustrations will suffice, although the case could be continued almost indefinitely. Redaction Criticism is the latest variant of the higher critical method. It is a reaction against Form Criticism, of which Rudolph Bultmann is perhaps the best known exponent.

In Form Criticism as it relates to the Gospels, the purpose is to get behind the words of Jesus to find what He really said, because most of what the Gospels say He said, He never really said. Redaction Criticism argues that the Gospel writers were not historians, but theologians. In developing their respective theologies, they put words into Jesus' mouth that He never said, and they ascribed to Him things He never did. In other words, they invented these things so as to give credence to the theology they wanted to develop.

If the Gospels are only theological and not historical and they tell us about things Jesus never said or did, then they are not trustworthy history and we're back trying to find the true canon of the Word of God in a Scripture that is both true and false. Once this principle is applied to the Gospel, the consequences are mindboggling. Normativity is forever lost, and anybody can make the Gospels say or not say anything they please.

The Purpose of God--Heilsgeschichte vs. Historie

Another straightjacket that is imposed on Scripture is the one that stresses the purpose of God which is to save men at the expense of fact and biblical inerrancy. This view effectively divides Scripture into two parts. Salvation history (what the Germans call heilsgeschichte) is what counts. History (historie) which deals with facts and figures, or the nuts and bolts, doesn't make any difference.

In this view, God infallibly accomplishes His purpose, which is to get men saved. He does it through an imperfect and fallible Word. No one, of course, should deny the fact that God is sovereign and that His purposes cannot be annulled. But to say that this is done through God's own inspired vehicle and that the inspired vehicle cannot be trusted in all of its parts is to deny any credible meaning to inspiration. But more than that.

If God is to infallibly accomplish His purpose, which is to save men, even that cannot come about unless there are some parts of the Bible that are both true in themselves and trustworthy. In other words, there must be statements in the Bible that are dependable. If there are not, then we are saved by a God we are not sure exists, who may or may not have had a son, who may or may not have been born of a virgin, who may or may not have died on a cross, who we think may possibly have risen from the dead, and on whom, possibly, we may or may not believe with no assurance that we have been saved. We only hope so.

Those who talk glibly about the infallible purpose of God must say there is either nothing at all in Scripture which is objectively true, or that there are parts of Scripture which are historical, true, and accurate. Whichever way they decide, they must end up either with no Scripture they can trust, or only some Scripture they can trust. If they limit what they can trust to some Scripture, they are right back with the advocates of the historical-critical methodology. They must find the Word of God in Scripture they can trust--i.e., the canon in the canon and this is the old subjectivity, for no two higher critics have ever agreed on what the canon in the canon is.

The Conclusion

This survey of the historical-critical method and illustrations of how it is used intentionally or unintentionally is indeed brief. Whole works should be devoted to this alone and able evangelical scholars should undertake the task. There can be no doubt, however, that the historical-critical methodology approaches the Bible in such a way that the infallibility or inerrancy of the Word of God cannot be upheld. This is why a large segment of the Christian church is seeking to find the canon in the canon. Because they have taught the historical-critical method, Scripture cannot be the Word of God. The Word of God is to be found in Scripture instead.

One critic of the historical-critical method said:

The point we are stressing is that the historical-critical method denies the role of transcendence in the history of Jesus as well as in the Bible as a whole, not as a result of scientific studies of the evidences, but because of its philosophical presuppositions about the nature of history...The historical-critical method excludes by definition that which I believe...(George E. Ladd, *Interpretation: A Journal of Theology* (Vol. XXV, No. 1, Jan. 1971, pp. 50,57).

It was Martin Luther who said there is a difference between the apostles and us. The apostles are the infallible teachers. We "may err and fall in faith," but not they.

According to this, the apostles in their statements in Scripture are infallible, because God has sent them to us as teachers. Inspiration here aims at the infallibility and the certainty of the faith which depends on this Word. Inspiration lifts Scripture above all human utterances as well as above all access by human criticism and, notwithstanding the fact that it was written by men, gives it the attributes and the preeminence of divine discourse. 'When God speaks through man, that is a far different thing than man himself speaking.' From this Luther concludes: 'So nothing but the divine words should be the first principles of Christians, but the words of all men are conclusions which are derived therefrom and must be led back to them and verified by them.' From here we arrive in a straight line at the convictions and formulations of late orthodoxy after Luther, where we read in the *Examen* of Hollaz or the *Epitome* of Calixt: 'Whatever Holy Scripture teaches is unfailingly true,' supplemented and supported by the thesis: 'In the most exact sense of the concept the Holy Scriptures are the Word of God' (Maier, op. cit., p. 65).

Answers to Life's Great Questions

We started our journey by posing four questions--Where did I come from? Who am I? Why am I here? and Where am I going? We have asserted that these are religious questions, and that in seeking to obtain answers to these questions we must be sure of two things: (1) We must be sure we have gone to the right source for our knowledge, and (2) We must be sure that the source from which we get our knowledge is itself telling us the truth.

We have said that the Bible is the source of our knowledge. It is the self-revelation of God, and has in it the answers to our basic questions. We have also said that the Bible is the only trustworthy source for our religious knowledge; that what is says can be trusted; and that the books that comprise the canon of the Old and New Testaments are true in all of their parts. They do not tell us lies; we can depend on what God says in them. How does the Bible answer the questions we have asked?

Answers – Where Did I Come From?--Origins

The question "Where did I come from?" has to do with my origins. At a very early age, most children ask, "Mommy, where did I come from?" The old story that the stork brings babies has given way to more realistic and factual accounts of how babies are conceived and are born. But these answers, while true enough, hardly

skim the surface of the persistent question how human life came into
being in the first place.

There are only a few possible answers to questions about man's
beginnings. We can say that we don't know. That's an answer, but it
is not a satisfactory one and most people go beyond it. After that, we
are left with two possible answers: that of the evolutionist and that
of the theist. We must remember, however, that there are two theistic answers to the question. We do have theistic evolutionists, and
special or immediate creationists.

The naturalist or evolutionist says that man is a part of nature
and is derived from pre-existing forms of animal life that have come,
in turn, from lower forms of life until we get back to the first cell.
The naturalist or evolutionist must then answer the question,
"Where did matter come from?" Phrased another way it is this, "If
man comes from nature through the evolutionary process, does matter have a beginning or has it always existed?" If it had a beginning,
then there must have been a first cause, and that first cause could
only have been God, whose existence naturalists and many evolutionists deny. Thus they must conclude that matter is eternal; there
was no beginning.

This viewpoint leads relentlessly to current atheistic existential-
ism, which has for its philosophical centerpiece the notion that life is
really meaningless—it makes no sense. And who would disagree with
this conclusion, given the underlying presupposition of atheism,
naturalism, and evolution? Where man came from, given this starting point, makes no difference anyhow. But this much we do know:
those who hold this view are not agnostic. They do have answers.
Professor George Gaylord Simpson of Harvard University says, "In
the post-Darwinian world another answer seems fairly clear: man is
responsible to himself and for himself" (*Science,* April 1, 1960,
p. 974). Harlow Shapley, director of the Harvard Observatory, said,
"Our God is humanity; our creed is effective participation in universal evolution" (*Beyond the Observatory,* Scribner, 1967, p. 171).
Professor Michael Ghiselin, University of California teacher, argues
that the evolutionary hypothesis makes supernaturalism obsolete
and God "a superfluous hypothesis" (*Science,* March 9, 1973,
p. 964). For them, man is part of nature, the beginning and end of
everything. He is here for a time but disappears without leaving more
than a trace; and has no continuing existence. He is simply a tempo-
rary manifestation of a higher form of life that is derived from lower
forms in an ascending scale.

Once we get beyond the "I don't know" answer and beyond the
naturalistic, atheistic answer we arrive at the third—and only

other—response to the question about man's origins, the theistic. This category as we have said, comprises two different schools of thought, special creationists and theistic evolutionists. They hold certain views in common, if they are Christians. Both regard man as creature and God as creator. Both agree that man was made for God, is responsible to God, is fallen, and needs redemption. From the theological perspective, the Christian theistic evolutionist opens himself to criticism that the special creationist does not face.

The first question theistic evolutionists must answer is whether matter is eternal. I know of no biblical theistic evolutionists who would argue for the eternity of matter. Thus, before matter there was only God, who is Spirit. If this be true, then in principle it would be possible for God to make man *ex nihilo*. The question would not be whether God *could* do this, but what God actually *did* do. It is here that theistic evolutionists tie man into the processes of nature.

Once science is introduced, it raises these questions in connection with man's origins: "What is the relationship between science and the Bible? What do we do if and when the so-called sure conclusions (which they are not) of science appear to contradict what we read in the Bible? Do we interpret the Bible so that it agrees with science or assume that the Bible is incorrect? But when the teaching of the Bible seemingly cannot be reconciled with science, do we then let science sit in judgment on the Bible or do we let the Bible sit in judgment on science?"

We have already said that we believe the Bible to be true in all of its parts, including those parts that speak about man's origins. The theistic evolutionary approach forces us into a hermeneutic (an interpretation) which regards the creation accounts as saga or myth rather than history and fact. This, in turn, does gross violence to other didactic portions of the Bible (e.g., Romans and Galatians) and creates other problems for which there are no answers. In the light of this, let's take a hard look at the special-creation view.

By special creation, we mean that man did not come from prior existing forms of life. The biblical account of Genesis does say that God fashioned man from the dust of the earth. It can be argued that dust had in it elements of life such as bacteria. This appears quite appropriate. But when we speak about creation from the dust of the earth and say man did not come from prior existing forms of life, the meaning is clear: man did not come from earlier forms of vertebrate life; he did not exist as a sub-human with a body similar to, or comparable to, Adam's body; Adam did not come from pre-existent animal life. Adam was an immediate creation of God, who fashioned him from the dust of the ground.

It is only fair to note that there are people who claim to be part of the community of faith who do not believe that the Adam of Genesis was a real person. Thus a man like John A.T. Robinson, an Anglican bishop and author of *Honest to God*, could write "...For Jesus, unlike Adam, *was* (his italics) a historical individual." (*Can We Trust the New Testament?* Grand Rapids: Eerdmans, 1977, p. 28).

Bishop Robinson says that "...had (Samuel Wilberforce and those who believed in special creation) won the day against Thomas Huxley and his allies, it would be impossible now to be a Christian *and* a scientist. The cause of the faith would have suffered irreparable damage--whereas in fact the stories of the creation *and the fall* (my italics) have now been liberated to become far more meaningful..." (*Ibid.*).

The Bible, which we believe, says that Adam was the first man; from him all future human life was to spring. Some say that the Hebrew word for Adam is a generic term meaning only "man." This is quite true, but it hardly proves anything significant. Virtually every human name springs from common words. David means "beloved"; Joshua means "Yahweh saves"; Henry means "ruler of the home"; Ralph means "wolf in counsel"; William means "desired helmet." For the name Adam to mean "man" hardly supposes that the word did not refer to a specific person who was the first of the human species.

Adam was regarded as the first man by the biblical writers. In First Chronicles 1, the genealogical table begins with Adam. Since the other people named in the table are obviously historical, who could deny that at least in the understanding of the chronicler, Adam was the beginner of the human race? In the New Testament genealogical table given by Luke (3:23 ff.), he traces the descendants of Jesus straight back to Adam, whom he designates as "the son of God."

The Apostle Paul builds his theology of redemption in Romans around the first and the second Adams. Jesus, for Paul, is the second Adam. The first Adam was the inhabitant of the Garden of Eden, our first ancestor through whom original sin came with all of its consequences. And it was the first man's sin that made necessary the second Adam's sacrifice on the cross of Calvary. To argue that the first Adam was a mythical figure while holding that the second Adam was true man, boggles the imagination and turns Scripture on its head. Moreover, if there was no first Adam, from whence did original sin come? The Bible allows for no other explanation for the intrusion of sin into the human race, once Adam is regarded as non-historical. Clearly, the Bible teaches that the entire human race springs from the first ancestor Adam, and that he came from God as a special and immediate creation.

What adds significance to the creation story is the account of Eve's beginnings. There are only two possible approaches to the Genesis account of Eve's creation: either it must be regarded as mythical, or it must be accepted as non-evolutionary in character. There is nothing in the biblical account that could make possible the evolution of Eve from previously existing animal forms. A deep sleep came upon Adam. God removed a rib from his rib cage. God fashioned Eve out of that rib that he took from Adam's body. No evolutionary proposal could possibly digest this information and make sense out of it from that standpoint.

What is clear is this, however: to accept the story of Eve's beginnings as given in Genesis in any historical sense is to knock the theory of evolution into a cocked hat. It brings to bear upon the creative process divine intervention, that drives the uniformitarian hypothesis and the endless eons of evolutionary development into the ground. If, in the face of the biblical data, the theistic evolutionist chooses to accept the hypothesis of some scientists, he at least should be conscious of what he is doing to the Bible in the process. He no longer makes it the source book for his knowledge of origins. In place thereof, he chooses the verdict of science and allows it to sit in judgment on the Bible rather than letting the Bible sit in judgment on science.

The long-held view derived from the Bible, that God created Adam immediately out of the dust of the ground, is by far the most acceptable explanation of the biblical data. It makes unnecessary the reduction of that data to myth or saga. It places the revelation of God above science, without creating problems for Christian scientists who accept the supernatural and regard miracles as part of the data of Scripture. And it answers the question, "Where did I come from?" in a way that makes sense and is in accord with the integrity of the Bible, whose inner harmony would be fractured by the acceptance of other viewpoints.

Who Am I?--Identity

The Bible states that man was made in the image of God. Adam was a moral and spiritual being. He was free and rational. He could think God's thoughts after Him. He had the power of contrary choice. Man is generically different from animals. Man has a body, but he also is spoken of as having a spirit and soul. So Paul prays for each Thessalonian believer that his or her "spirit and soul and body be kept sound and blameless at the coming of our Lord Jesus Christ" (1 Thessalonians 5:23).

The Bible tells us that Adam and Eve set up housekeeping in the Garden of Eden, and God provided everything they needed. They were commanded to tend the Garden and enjoy its fruit. They were rightly related to their Creator and lived in innocence without any knowledge or experience of sin. It was truly a paradise which was theirs to enjoy forever. But since they were moral creatures and had the power of contrary choice, God made it possible for them to walk forever in fellowship with Him, or break the relationship.

The Genesis account states that God planted many trees in the Garden of Eden. But only two trees are named: the tree of life, and the tree of the knowledge of good and evil. Everything belonged to Adam and Eve except one thing. They were forbidden by God to eat of the fruit of the tree of the knowledge of good and evil. They were warned that this would be the sole test of their obedience, of their fealty, and of their loyalty to God and His one command. They were not forbidden to eat of the fruit of the tree of life. So long as they obeyed the one restriction laid on them by God they were free, holy, rightly related to their Creator, and would be able to live without fear, without sickness, without pain, without sorrow, and without death.

The story of Adam and Eve is your story and mine. It is the story of the disobedience of our first parents and their fall into the abyss. They became what they were not when first they were placed in the Garden. They were separated from God and consigned to expulsion from their paradise. It was indeed fitting for John Milton to title his epic poem *Paradise Lost*. But the loss of the Garden was only a small fraction of what they suffered for their disobedience. To each was given a sentence, and to both was given, in addition to penalties of which we shall speak in a moment, the sentence of death. But before they died they were to suffer or smart for their disobedience.

Eve was told that she would have pain in childbearing and that her husband was to rule over her. The pain of childbearing has been as nothing compared to the subordination that has been the lot of women to their husbands ever since. Indeed, many women have suffered under this yoke. Today, many wish to be delivered from it. And when they seek to do so, they are only repeating the sin of their mother Eve. What God said in Genesis about Eve's subordination to her husband is repeated by Paul in Ephesians. To allege either that the Genesis account is myth, or that the penalty does not apply to believers in this age, is to destroy Scripture as normative.

To Adam was given the bad news that the earth was now cursed; thorns and thistles should abound; in the sweat of his brow would he labor for his food and for the food of his wife which he was to supply. They were then expelled from the Garden, given clothes to wear, and forbidden to eat of the tree of life which was now guarded with a flaming sword so that they could not eat. The penalties attached to Adam were different from those given to Eve but they were no less onerous and men have sought deliverance from them to this very hour.

But the full penalty for Adam's transgression included the promise of death. He would suffer while he lived and he would also die. He had come from the earth and he would be swallowed up by the earth when his dead body was returned to it. But there was a greater penalty yet. He would not only suffer death; he would be separated from God, and this because he was now a sinner. This is *my* story (and yours) when I ask the question, "Who am I?" I am made in the image of God, but that image has been defaced and marred and I am lost and undone, without hope in this world or in the world to come. I am a lost soul wandering in the wilderness. I cannot find my way out. Indeed, I am a son of God because He made me. But I have abandoned my father's home, given up my patrimony, and I have become a wanderer over the face of the earth. I have no certain dwelling place. I am filled with fear. I experience tragedy and sorrow. I find that life is bondage and death does not solve my problems. O wretched man that I am, who shall deliver me from my sad estate?

God has disclosed my identity to me in the Bible. He has sketched for me my sad situation. I am the prodigal who gave up everything in exchange for something I thought was desirable. I discovered that I got nothing for my pains, while I had lost everything. I can't live with myself. I can't live with anybody else. I'm like a ship without a crew on the high seas amid a violent storm. Even if I had a place to go, I do not know where it is, or how to get there.

Is this *all* the Bible has to tell me about myself? Is there no hope for me in the midst of my darkness? "If you made me like yourself, O God, have you abandoned me forever?" Glory be to the God who condemned me and whose strong arm is set against me. He, says the Bible, loves me still. He seeks after me. He wants me to come home. And this has to do with the question, "Why am I here?"

Why Am I Here?--Purpose

I am here because God put me here. And God's intention for me is that I should come to know Him who made me and is the author of everlasting life. God wants me to be restored to fellowship with Him and to live forever. He wants me to recover the Paradise that Adam and Eve lost. He wants me to worship and to adore Him. He wants me to enjoy my Creator forever.

Adam was kept from the tree of life. But God has made Jesus Christ His Son the tree of life for me. There is a sense in which I am just like Adam except that the situation is completely reversed. Adam was a saint who became a sinner. I am a sinner who needs to become a saint. Adam was innocent. I am not. Adam needed no redeemer. I do. Adam only had to keep from eating the fruit of the tree of the knowledge of good and evil. I have eaten. Adam was not separated from God. I am. But God has left me with a choice. I must eat of the tree of life, if I am to regain what I lost in Adam. I am alive, so this remains a possibility for me so long as I live. I am here and faced with life's greatest decision. This is what the Bible is all about. It is my Book of hope. It is my Book of freedom. It is my Book of liberation. It is the Book that brings me to the tree of life.

I am here that I may experience the grace of God in my life. I am here so that what Jesus Christ did on Calvary when He died for my sins may bring about my deliverance. The Bible tells me that God was in Christ reconciling the world unto Himself. This Book tells me that God so loved the world that He gave His only begotten son. This Book tells me that by faith in Jesus Christ I can inherit the gift of everlasting life. This Book opens the doorway to heaven and makes possible what no other book and no other religion can do. This Book, which is the Word of God written, leads straight to the Word of God incarnate.

Jesus is the tree of life. If I eat of His body and drink of His blood I shall get back the life that I lost in Adam. If I do this, I shall discover that life has meaning and purpose. I shall become a child of God. I shall become a joint heir with Jesus Christ in His kingdom. I shall have all that I need for the living of this life, and for that life which is to come. I am here that I might choose Jesus. I am here so that others can know from my life and my testimony that what Jesus did for me He can do for them.

I am here to do battle with Satan, the archenemy of God and Jesus Christ. I am here to fight the good fight and to lay hold of eternal life. I have been promised that in this life I shall have tribulation. There are foes to face; there are battles to be fought and won; there are fields to be conquered. But there is a power available which makes it possible for me to do what I have been commanded to do. In brief, I am here to glorify God. And how is it possible for me to do this? First, I glorify God when I believe His Word and come to

Jesus Christ for salvation and for restoration to His fellowship. Second, I glorify God when I commit my life without reservation to God for whatever it is that He wants me to be and what He wants to do with me. Third, I glorify God when I am under the control of His Holy Spirit. Fourth, I glorify God when I walk in obedience to His commandments and they are not grievous to me.

What is the answer to the last of life's great, great questions, "Where am I going?" We all know that death is inevitable. We all know that no U-Haul ever follows a hearse. We cannot take anything with us. We leave this earth as we came into it--empty-handed. What happens when we die?

What Happens When I Die?--Destiny

The Bible opens the door for us to peer into eternity. It paints a graphic picture of life after death. It is a black and white sketch of opposites. The contrast is so enormous that it is frightening. We are told that the hereafter consists of two places. One is good; the other is bad. The differences between them are such that no one could possibly mistake one for the other. There is a larger and a smaller aspect to the situation.

The larger or cosmic aspect of the hereafter involves two persons: God and Satan. There is a terrible warfare going on between them. It is a struggle of life and death. At this moment, life consists in a dualism. There is a malignant force headed up by Satan that is evil. Evil overcame good in the Garden of Eden. We have already mentioned the consequences that befell Adam and Eve because they sided with Satan rather than with God. But there is more to it than that.

Adam and Eve lost something when they sinned. Satan gained something. It is important that we see this. Satan, by Adam's sin, wrested control of the planet earth from God. It became his planet. He is its sovereign lord. It is, for a while, his domain. But his control is not uncontested. God has entered enemy territory in the person of Jesus Christ, God's Son, who has invaded earth for the purpose of regaining control. The Son was sent by His Father to win the day, and He will give this planet back to His Father when the victory is won at last. Let it be said, however, that the earth is enemy territory.

The work of Jesus is twofold. It has to do with people and territory. For a king to be a king he must have a country and people. Jesus has come to win people to His side. For without people there can be no kingdom. And He has come to regain possession of the planet that Satan has seized by force, for without territory there can be no kingdom.

There are three events related to the work of Jesus. The first has to do with the incarnation. Jesus had to become man. He had to secure a beachhead in the enemy's territory. He came as a baby in Bethlehem. And Satan's follower, King Herod, sought to stamp out the infant Jesus by his slaughter of the innocents. But he failed in his attempt.

The second pivotal event in the life of Jesus was the Cross of Calvary. Here we encounter what appears to be a shocking paradox. The good one dies. The Devil seems to have gained the victory. But a great mystery is wrapped up in this event. The death of Jesus is essential to regaining the Paradise that was lost. By His death, He conquered death and from His death there flows endless life!

At Calvary, Jesus dealt a deathblow to Satan. In principle, the battle is already won. In fact Satan has been mortally wounded, but he is not yet finally overcome. In his dying moments, he thrashes about seeking to devour all he can. He knows he must lose control and possession of this planet. But he intends to carry with him in his death as many of God's human creatures as he can. He wants company in that final resting place which shall be his.

The earth at this point in history is a battleground. The whole creation groans waiting for its deliverance. The souls of men hang in the balance, and whether they will side with Satan or go with God is the great question. Men, so long as they live in the flesh, are in a state of probation. But when death comes their probation is ended. Their destiny is determined. Their condition is fixed forever. What happens to men after death is determined *before* they die, not after.

It is Jesus who says clearly that when men die they go either to one place or another. In Luke 16:19 ff., Jesus told the story about the rich man and Lazarus. The contrast between the two men while they were on earth is quite extreme. The contrast between them after death is more extreme. One went to "heaven" and the other to "hell." These words require some explanation. But before we consider them, a few observations are in order.

Jesus teaches us in this story that immediately upon death everyone goes to one of the two places. He teaches that the dead are conscious and are aware of where they are. He indicates that the place to which a man goes is fixed, and there can be no change in a person's estate after death. One place consists in unbroken suffering; the other consists in unbroken felicity and joy.

What Jesus talks about in this account has to do with the intermediate estate. For we learn from other Scripture there is a resurrection of both the saved and the unsaved. And there is a judgment seat of Christ for believers at which rewards will be handed out. There is a judgment of the wicked dead which is called the judgment of the Great White Throne. In the period between death and the resurrection of the dead, when body and soul are reunited, is this intermediate estate--a place of sorrow and a place of happiness, but not the final abode of the saved and the lost.

The final resting place of the people of God is the New Jerusalem, a prepared city that shall come down from God out of heaven. It is described in Revelation 21:9 ff. In this city there is "a pure river of water of life." And there is "the tree of life," the same tree that was in the Garden of Eden. The people of God shall live forever in the New Jerusalem. The Lamb is the light, the gates are always open, and nothing enters that can ever defile it.

The final resting place of the wicked dead is the lake of fire where the Devil, the beast, and the false prophet shall go. Here they who have tormented their victims shall themselves "be tormented day and night for ever and ever" (Rev. 20:10). So far as men are concerned, those whose names are not written in the Lamb's book of life shall be cast into the same lake of fire. This is the final resting place of the wicked.

God has set before men life or death; heaven or hell; God or Satan. Where men go depends on what they do with Jesus, on which side they cast their lot in the dualism between good and evil. Good will triumph, and evil will be contained forever. The present contingent dualism will yield to a divine monism when the cosmos once more will be undefiled. God, we see, will not only save men; He will also redeem His lost creation and renovate it. He will bring it back to its pristine glory.

Men have been given the power of choice. They can flee to Jesus as their refuge or they can follow Satan. But over the portals of the doors that lead to heaven and to hell are the signposts that warn men about the consequences that follow their decision. Men can choose either life or death, but there is one thing they cannot do. They cannot change the facts. There is life and there is death; there is a heaven and there is a hell; there is good and there is evil; there is a redeemer and there is a destroyer.

Thoughtful people may ask this question, "Suppose there is no life after death?" "What difference will it make what I do here, if there is nothing hereafter?" This question can be answered two ways. First, the Bible categorically asserts there *is* a life after death. If the Bible is not correct, then it makes little difference. But the truth of the Bible has been corroborated by an undeniable fact. Jesus Christ rose from the dead and is alive forevermore. The Christian faith stands or falls on His resurrection. If He lives we shall live also.

If He did not rise from the dead, we will not be raised from the dead. It is as simple as that.

There is one other thought that is important when men consider Jesus. If I choose Jesus and at the end of life discover (I don't believe I will, but I ask it because some do look at things from this perspective) that I am mistaken, what have I lost? I have followed a pathway of rectitude that would commend itself to any thoughtful person. I have lived a life of sharing, of helpfulness to my neighbor. I have raised my children to be good citizens, to do their duty, to obey the law. I have found satisfaction within and without. What, then, have I lost? Nothing.

But if I go my own way, do my own thing, reject Jesus Christ and come to the end of life only to discover the Bible is true and Jesus Christ really is the way, the truth, and the life, what then? I have lost everything. And it is too late. Those who live for Jesus, if they're mistaken, have lost nothing; but those who don't, have lost everything. Why should a prudent man gamble that the Bible is wrong, when there are a thousand reasons to believe it is right? And if I have a chance to gain everything and lose nothing by coming to Jesus, why should I not come?

Plainly, there is a heaven to gain and a hell to shun. But where we go when life is over depends on whether we respond for or against the Son of God.

A black preacher from America's southland caught the heart of the Christian answer to the question, "What happens when I die?" He saw the angel of death visit the home of one of God's children. And so he wrote:

And God said: Go down, Death, go down,
Go down to Savannah, Georgia,
Down in Yamacraw,
And find Sister Caroline.
She's borne the burden and heat of the day,
She's labored long in my vineyard,
And she's tired--
She's weary.
Go down, Death, and bring her to me.

While we were watching round her bed,
She turned her eyes and looked away,
She saw what we couldn't see:
She saw Old Death. She saw Old Death
Coming like a falling star.
But Death didn't frighten Sister Caroline;

He looked to her like a welcome friend.
And she whispered to us: I'm going home,
And she smiled and closed her eyes.

Weep not, weep not,
She is not dead;
She's resting in the bosom of Jesus.

And I say to you who put your trust in Jesus--whatever may befall you in the days or years to come:
Weep not, weep not,
We will not die.
We will rest forever in the bosom of Jesus.
Amen.

The Conclusion of the Matter

We are close to the end of our journey. One more subject needs exploration. In a way, it is almost as vital as the subjects we have been discussing, although it cannot stand by itself. It requires the underpinning of what has been established already. We may think of this as a house that we build on a secure foundation.

The Bible *is* the Word of God and is without error in all of its parts. We believe this because the Bible itself makes this claim. We believe it because of the witness of Jesus who is the Word of God incarnate. We have seen that the Jews of Jesus' day believed it. We have noted that the Church through the ages believed it. We perceive that it has been demonstrated by fulfilled prophecy, by the witness of the Holy Spirit, by the spade of the archaeologist, and by the testimonies of multiplied millions of professing believers across the long centuries since Pentecost. But we must also remember that the demons believe all of this too, and they are not saved.

Men can have head knowledge without heart faith. They can profess belief but have no spiritual life. They can know and hold to something without it ever becoming a part of their real inner life. Talking about a trustworthy Bible can be an exercise in gymnastics, a scholastic approach to a problem, just as scientists approach problems in physics and chemistry. If we choose to do so, we can put the Bible in the laboratory and deal with it as we deal with other books. We can find out what the Apostle Paul teaches about this or that or some other matter. We can conclude that his teaching indeed is what true Christians have believed for ages. None or all of these proves we have saving faith. Therefore, we cannot leave the subject of a trustworthy Bible without declaring that there is more to the Christian faith than an infallible Book. What are we talking about?

A verse of Scripture in Ezra throws light on the matter (7:10). It says that "Ezra had set his heart to study the law of the Lord, and to do it, and to teach his statutes and ordinances in Israel." What does this say to us?

The Things We Must Do – Know the Word of God

Knowing the Word of God has a twofold point of reference. It is essential to know the Word of God for salvation. This is primary. But this does not mean that we must know everything that is found in Scripture. At the same time, no one can be converted without knowing something about the Word of God. "Faith cometh by hearing, and hearing by the word of God" (Romans 10:17). This raises the question what we must know about God in order to be saved.

When we talk about salvation, of necessity we are talking about the minimum knowledge that we must possess in order to become Christians. Often, we think that we really know or have heard the full content of the Gospel when we have heard that Christ died for our sins, was buried, and rose again from the dead the third day (see 1 Corinthians 15:3,4). However, we must not forget that even when we know this, there are other truths that are implied. We must believe in God. We must believe that we are sinners and need Christ for salvation. We must at least hold that the death of Jesus did something for us that makes salvation possible. And we must believe that Jesus, whose body lay in the tomb for three days, has come back to life. Quite apparently, there are theological implications in all of these things that have captured the imaginations and minds of laymen and scholars, who have tried to plumb the depths of these articles of the Christian faith without ever having struck bottom. No one ever has fully exhausted, or ever will, all that is comprehended in them.

At the time a person comes to saving faith in Jesus Christ, there are many things he need not know. This does not mean that these things are secondary or that salvatory doctrines outshine everything else. The second coming of Jesus is a prime doctrine of the Christian faith. Yet an unbeliever can be saved without ever hearing anything about the return of the Lord. He may never have heard of the virgin birth of Jesus. He may never have heard of the doctrine of the Trinity. The point we make here is that no one can be saved without knowing something, although he does not need to know everything. But knowledge alone does not save.

Knowledge that is imparted to us must filter through our heads, and we must agree that we believe the knowledge or that we do not believe it. Salvation requires that we believe that Christ died for our sins and rose again for our justification. But believing these things leaves us short of eternal life, if belief is not followed by personal appropriation. We must also note that when we claim we believe these salvatory truths we are saying, as a minimum, that we believe what the Bible asserts about these things. We must trust the Bible for this. Believing these truths and trusting the Bible must be followed by an act of will or of choice. This is volitional. We must lay hold of Jesus Christ. So saving faith includes knowledge, intellectual assent to the salvatory facts, and a reaching out to lay hold of Jesus Christ. When these three things take place we are saved. We know that some Christians include water baptism as one of the necessary steps in the salvatory process. Certainly, the Bible commands us to submit to water baptism. Few will deny this. The tough question is whether someone can be saved without water baptism, as the dying thief was saved at Calvary. Baptists, for example, believe that water baptism is an act of obedience that occurs subsequent to regeneration. Some Lutheran and Episcopalian brothers believe that water baptism is essential to the salvatory process. It may help to resolve the problem if Christians agree that those who do come to Jesus should be baptized in water. Then it becomes less important to decide whether they are saved before or during or after the baptism by water.

Here we are deeply concerned, not about the amount of knowledge a person must have in order to be saved, but what he does *with* the Bible *after* he has been saved. Ezra was a true believer. The Scripture says he "set his heart to study the law of the Lord." Whereas in salvation choice comes after knowledge, here knowledge comes after choice. Ezra set himself to know the Word of God. It was a deliberate decision on his part and rose out of obedience to the faith which demands that Scripture be studied. In 2 Timothy 2:15, the Scripture says, "Do your best to present yourself to God as one approved, a workman who has no need to be ashamed, rightly handling the word of truth." In the LIVING BIBLE that verse is translated, "Work hard so that God can say to you, 'Well done.' Be a good workman, one who does not need to be ashamed when God examines your work. Know what his Word says and means."

This particular verse says that the Christian is a workman. And the word is used in connection with his study of the Word of God. The Christian is cautioned that he will be judged according to his labors, and the basis on which the judgment will be made is how well he knows the Word of the living God. We may conclude that once a person becomes a Christian, he or she has an ongoing responsibility to read, to study, and to know the Word of God. This is not optional; it is obligatory. But it is not to be thought of as a chore. It is work, of course, but not a chore. It pays off rich dividends because it brings the believer closer to God, it helps to transform his life, and it provides him with the spiritual food he needs to grow in grace. More is lost by failing to study the Word of God than most believers imagine.

Gaining proficiency in the Word of God can be done a number of ways. Sitting under the ministry of a good Bible teacher in a Sunday School is one way; listening to the Word of God preached in worship services is another; studying the Word of God by oneself is still another. Bible study groups have become popular in American life more recently. This is good indeed, but it tells us that God's people somehow feel there is a lack in their lives. They know something is missing and they do not quite know what it is. The thousands of home Bible studies that meet weekly do help those who are eager to increase their knowledge of God.

The student should obtain a good concordance, a solid evangelical commentary such as Matthew Henry, and a topical index book that provides information about Bible themes such as justification, regeneration, etc. A good Bible dictionary is also a basic tool. A study Bible such as the *Harper Study Bible* is good for following each book of the Bible in outlined form, for the cross-references, and for the footnotes that supply important information immediately as the Bible is being read. With these few essential books in hand, the Christian should read through the Bible at least once each year. One way to do this is to read one book at a time. The student can start with Genesis and when that book has been read go to the Gospel according to St. Matthew; then go back to Exodus, then to Mark and so on until the Bible has been read through completely. In the average Bible, by reading five pages a day the student can easily finish the whole Bible in a year's time, and it need not take more than fifteen or twenty minutes a day to do this.

We speak to God via prayer; God speaks to us via the Bible. We should let God speak to us before we speak to Him. And He will speak by His Spirit as we read His Word. In the history of Israel, the Word of God was often misplaced or given no place in the lives of the people. Whenever this happened, they fell into sin. That is why the Bible says, "Thy word have I hid in mine heart, that I might not sin against thee" (Psalm 119:11). We can understand why there might have been a famine of the Word of God in the Old Testament times. But most Christians today have a copy of the Bible, and most of them can read the Bible. For some, it is the most unread book in the house, with news programs on TV and newspapers occupying more of the Christians' time than the Word of God itself. In some places around the world, copies of the Bible are hard to come by. Governments in some countries will not permit the Bible to be printed or distributed. The people who do not have Bibles are to be pitied and prayed for. But what of the multitudes who *do* have Bibles? There is no excuse for their delinquency.

If the first step in the Christian life is to *know* the Word of God, the second step is to *do* the will of God.

Do the Word of God

From the beginning, God dealt with Adam on a twofold basis. He was supposed to do some things and he was forbidden to do others. The same is true with respect to the Ten Commandments. They contain positive and negative commands. The first five speak of things that God tells men they must do. The last five constitute prohibitions of things they are to shun. Some people suppose the prohibitions prevent them from enjoying good things. So they complain against God and His commandments as though He has placed unnecessary restrictions on them. This is not so.

Everything written in Scripture by way of prohibition exists for the benefit of men. We live in a moral universe. It has laws of its own. Those who break the laws of God with regard to the universe shall be broken by those laws when they disobey them. To warn men not to build houses on the slopes of a volcanic mountain that could erupt any moment is negative indeed. But it is merciful and good, especially if men do not know that the volcano may erupt.

It is equally good for California to place signs on the exits of its six-lane highways warning motorists not to enter them. It is not designed to keep them from the beneficial use of the highways. It is intended to save their lives and the lives of others. Horrible accidents and many deaths have occurred when motorists have entered what they thought were entrances to the highways when they were exits.

The road of life has its exits and its entrances. God has erected warning signs along the way for the protection of those who travel the highway. They are not arbitrary signs invented to discomfort men. They are for their good.

When the Bible tells men not to get drunk the warning is for men's good. No one with a sound mind could suppose that drunkenness is a blessing. When God warns men not to steal, He is telling men that the universe is set up so that those who steal will reap evil rather than good. Fornication, adultery, and homosexual activities are wrong in principle. The doing of these forbidden things produces adverse results in the lives of those who engage in such activities, even as sometimes it ruins innocent victims who do not participate in these activities but who are nonetheless hurt by those who do them. The law against murder bespeaks the fact that God sets a high price on the sacredness and sanctity of life. And it is designed to protect those who themselves would never commit murder but who might be murdered by those who are evil. The awfulness of murder springs from the fact that men bear the *imago dei*, so that when someone kills another he is striking at God through the creature. This is a great sin, and the universe is set up so that those who murder will find they cannot escape the consequences. Anybody who thinks for a moment must realize that murder would be intrinsically wrong even if there were no divine or human sanctions against it by God, or by the nations of the world.

Telling the truth is the glue that holds society together. Every decent relationship of life is based upon trust. The wife trusts her husband that he will not cheat on her. A friend trusts another friend that what he tells him is true. A child trusts his father that he speaks the truth. There could be no satisfactory business dealings without the element of trust. God has not forbidden lying to keep something good from men. He has commanded men to tell the truth because a society based on lying must eventually collapse of its own weight.

Christians are called by God to do what God tells them to do in His Word. Anyone who professes to believe that the Bible is the completely trustworthy Word of God and then fails to do the will of God as expressed in Scripture is either a hypocrite, a backslidden believer, an ignorant follower who does not know the Word of God, or an unregenerate person who has deceived himself into thinking he is what he is not. There can be no excuse for any true believer who does not do the will of God. Jesus Himself said that if anyone has a question about biblical doctrine, the way to discover whether it is true lies in the pathway of obedience, not in the pathway of intellectual theorizing. He said, "If any man's will is to do his will, he shall know whether the teaching is from God, or whether I am speaking on my own authority" (John 7:17). The pathway to the fuller and deeper Christian life is not to question Scripture nor to disbelieve it; the right path to follow is to obey it. And when we do this we know the doctrine, and we gain faith to believe more deeply than ever in the truth of the living Word of God.

Teach the Word of God

Ezra and Nehemiah were two prominent leaders who helped the return of the Jews to Jerusalem after the Babylonian Captivity. Both of them realized the need to instruct the returned remnant in the law of God.

Truly, no one can rightly teach the law of God if he does not know it himself. Nor can he do this with effectiveness if he does not practice what he professes. But it is not sufficient to know and to do the law of God. It must be taught and proclaimed as widely as possible.

Of **Ezra,** the Scripture says that he "had prepared his heart...to teach in Israel the statutes and judgment." Surely this suggests that what he was about to do was not unplanned, nor was he unprepared. It was not happenstance. Rather, it was based upon the conviction that teaching the Word of God is one of the highest priorities. If the Word is taught, it will be effective. Sometimes the immediate response may appear to be small. But if it isn't done there will be no response.

Ezra followed in the tradition, the life style, and the injunction of Moses with respect to teaching the Word of God.

Moses has been called the "law giver" but it is more accurate to say he was the "law receiver." It was the Word of God, not the word of Moses, for Ezra speaks of the law of Moses as that "which the Lord God of Israel had given" (Ezra 7:6).

Before his death, Moses blessed the tribes of Israel and made clear that the Levites were responsible for teaching God's people His law. Moses, of course, was himself from the tribe of Levi, and it was this tribe that God set apart for the priesthood. The Levites, beginning with Aaron whose descendants were to constitute the priesthood, were to teach the law.

In his last speech, Moses said of the Levites, "They shall teach Jacob thy judgments, and Israel thy law" (Deuteronomy 33:10).

In those days, the teaching of the law of God was far more significant than today for a simple reason. Whereas virtually every believer can obtain a Bible today, there were very few copies of the law of God available in Moses' day. Therefore, those who had the written Word of God were the only source from which the teaching could be expected to come.

What Moses said at the end of his life was only repetition of his constant life attitude. More than that, he regarded the ministry of teaching to include parents, who were to transmit their own religious knowledge to their children. And their teaching did more than simply acquaint them with the law of God. That law, or those commandments of God, were enforced by parents on their children.

In Deuteronomy when the Great Commandment is given--Thou shalt love the Lord thy God--it is followed by this statement which is attributed to God, "And these words, which I command thee this day, shall be in thine heart: and thou shalt teach them diligently unto thy children, and shalt talk of them when thou sittest in thine house, and when thou walkest by the way, and when thou liest down, and when thou risest up" (Deut. 6:6,7).

According to Moses, the law of God was not just a Saturday affair. It was an every day, all day, affair. It was central, not peripheral, to all of life.

When **Nehemiah** came back to Jerusalem, he joined hands with Ezra to rebuild Jerusalem. And he records in his book how the people gathered together and were instructed in the law of God.

We are told in chapter eight of Nehemiah that "the people gathered themselves together as one man into the street." "They spake unto Ezra the scribe to bring the book of the law of Moses."

Ezra "stood upon a pulpit of wood" and read the law. When he opened it to read, the people stood. But he and his helpers did more than simply read the law. They expounded it and applied it. They "caused the people to understand the law" and they "gave the sense and caused them to understand the reading."

It is difficult to conceive of any greater tragedy in life than when the Word of God is absent. And we might add when the Word of God is diluted, abused, and misused.

The Holy Spirit used the prophet **Amos** to pronounce the judgment of God against Israel for its backsliding. Part of the promised judgment had to do with the Word of God. Amos said:

Behold the days come, saith the Lord God, that I will send a famine in the land, not a famine of bread, nor a thirst for water, but of hearing the words of the Lord. And they shall wander from sea to sea, and from the north even to the east, they shall run to and fro to seek the word of the Lord, and shall not find it.

Is this not a startling statement for those of us who have the Word of God but do not want it? What then will be our sad condition when the time comes that we want the Word of God, and we find we can't have it? And there will be no one to teach it to us.

The office of teacher in **Jesus'** day was highly exalted. Jesus Himself is spoken of as the world's greatest teacher. We do not think of Jesus as a preacher. There is a difference between the ministry of preaching and the ministry of teaching. Preaching has to do with proclamation; teaching has to do with instruction, and constitutes a larger field of endeavor.

When Jesus sent forth His disciples the Scripture says, "They went out and *preached* that men should repent" (Mark 6:12). But when it speaks about Jesus it usually says something like this, "He opened His mouth, and taught them" (Matthew 5:2); "He taught in their synagogues" (Luke 4:15); "as He was teaching" (Luke 5:17); "He taught them as one that had authority" (Mark 1:22). He did preach to be sure, but most of His ministry was a teaching one.

The ministry of **Paul** was, in a major sense, a teaching ministry. The books of Romans and Galatians are examples of this. It was Paul who laid down the dictum which underlies the work of every theological seminary, Christian college, Bible college, and Bible institute. He wrote to Timothy, "And the things thou hast heard of me among many witnesses, the same commit to faithful men, who shall be able to teach others also" (2 Timothy 2:2).

In this statement, Paul alludes to his own teaching ministry. The word "also" identifies all future teachers with him and his ministry of teaching.

In what does teaching consist? He has in mind the teaching of the Word of God in all of its beauty, purity, depth, and power.

We can be sure that bad teaching will have bad consequences, even as good teaching will be beneficial. The absence of teaching is baneful too. And many a pulpit around the world is useless, because the Word of God is not expounded and the people are not taught.

The Last Word

God's people must know and do the Word of God. They must also propagate that Word by their teaching. Parents are to teach their children; husbands and wives are to learn from each other; pulpits and Sunday Schools are to sound forth the excellencies of the Word; Christian schools of all kinds are to validate their existence through the taught Word.

Those who teach must themselves be taught. Their greatest teacher is the Holy Spirit of whom Jesus says, "Howbeit when he, the Spirit of truth is come, he will guide you into all truth: for he shall not speak of himself; but whatsoever he shall hear, that shall he speak: and he will shew you things to come. He will glorify me" (John 16:13,14). "The Holy Ghost...shall teach you all things, and bring all things to your remembrance, whatsoever I have said unto you" (John 14:26).

Every road that the teacher walks leads to the same destination, for the goal of all teaching is to bring us face to face with Jesus. All things written in Moses and the prophets and all things written in the New Testament pertain to Him.

There are only two Words of God: the Word of God written, and the Word of God incarnate, Jesus Christ. Both Words are intimately and forever interrelated. Whenever one is denigrated or diluted, the other suffers as well. A famine in the hearing of the Word of God written is a famine of the Word of God incarnate.

"O Spirit of the living God, illumine my mind, and my teacher be. Let me see Jesus in thy Word, for to know Him aright of whom thy Word speaks is life eternal."

Amen.